TAMING THE FOUR-HEADED DRAGON

A Must-Have Guide for Financial Advisors:
Get the Sales Growth YOU Need, the Clients
YOU Want—All with Limited Time

BILL WALTON

iUniverse LLC
Bloomington

TAMING THE FOUR-HEADED DRAGON
A Must-Have Guide for Financial Advisors: Get the Sales Growth
YOU Need, the Clients YOU Want—All with Limited Time

iUniverse books may be ordered through booksellers or by contacting:

iUniverse LLC
1663 Liberty Drive
Bloomington, IN 47403
www.iuniverse.com
1-800-Authors (1-800-288-4677)

ISBN: 978-1-4917-1839-1 (sc)
ISBN: 978-1-4917-1840-7 (hc)
ISBN: 978-1-4917-1841-4 (e)

Library of Congress Control Number: 2014901885

Printed in the United States of America.

iUniverse rev. date: 02/27/2014

CONTENTS

ACKNOWLEDGMENTS

Writing this book and working as a coach and trainer is truly a gift. I love what I do and have so many people to thank. When you get to the point where you think you're ready to write a book, you reflect back on your own experience and the people who helped you along the way. First and foremost, to my parents Bill and Marilyn Walton, thanks for all your support. I never would have decided to go into business for myself and take the risks I did without your belief in me. Dad, you never let me quit, and to this day, I "select and never settle." Mom, you are always ready with a kind word.

I also had great managers who believed in me and gave me all the coaching I needed to succeed. Thanks to George Cleary at Nestle Foods, Bob Munroe at Tambrands, and Bobbi Smith at the Forum Corporation, three of the best sales managers I ever had. They supported me and helped me see opportunity where I couldn't. To John Orvos, nationally recognized sales coach and author of *The Four Faces of Sales*, thanks for helping me understand the power of sleuthing and the way to sell with the greatest tool of all, the client's spoken words. You're a great friend, and I'm so glad we met.

To my clients, thank you all for your appreciation of my process and trust in what we could accomplish together. I love working with you, and thanks for letting me make my hobby a career. To Charlie Balducci at Merrill Lynch, who introduced me to the world of the financial advisor, thanks for your vision and seeing the role I could play in your wonderful profession. Thanks also to the folks at American Century for making ProDirect such a large part of your value-added efforts.

And to my wife, Amy, and daughter, Juliet, your undying support and willingness to celebrate even the smallest accomplishment makes all the difference to me every day.

INTRODUCTION

Hopefully you were curious about the title when you chose this book. While it lends an author a lot of creative avenues, the concept is very real. Present company included, we are all in professional services sales. We have to sell, manage what we win, have a relevant point of view, and deal with the administration that comes with it.

For the last twenty years, I've been helping clients and colleagues leverage sales processes and messaging to land more clients. During much of that time, I've been selling expensive, multifaceted consulting projects with long sales cycles. While big deals are great, you still need to hit quota. I learned early on that, if I were going to be successful, I had to find a way to balance the need to close now with the need to cultivate larger, longer-term relationships. Often this balancing act made me money in addition to my pure selling skill.

When running a professional services business as you do as a financial advisor (FA), you need to balance the time and energies of four critical functions: serving existing clients, attracting new prospects, engaging in thought leadership, and administering the practice. The success of the advisors I've coached has come as a direct result of how they've balanced these four distinct energies. For some, it comes naturally. For others, it's a conscious effort.

In the context of running a practice, I call these energies "dragons." At any given time, these dragons compete with one another and can take away focus from the activities that drive your practice. Each is necessary to run an effective book, but depending on your evolution as an FA, your pressures can be very different. For example, if you're an advisor new to the business, you have to be careful not to spend too much time managing the clients in your book. It sounds counterintuitive, but at this stage, it's all about pipeline build. For the seasoned FA, you need to provide high levels of service and value to your existing clients, a source of referral support and thus new client asset growth.

There is an inherent time management–prospecting connection in managing these four energies as well. A current client of mine says, "You have to manage your time from the inside out." This means you can't apply static time management disciplines outside of the context of the work that needs to be done. In other words, prospecting isn't linear. For example, you may call a prospect at noon, and she's not there. Your best writing and creativity might not hit you until four o'clock in the afternoon.

And right after an exhausting day following the markets, it might not be the best time to get on the phone and book appointments. That's why we treat time management and prospecting together.

You have to manage your time from the inside out.

The other energy connection is the link to your thought leadership, your point of view and process around developing plans for your ideal client type. This thought leadership is not market dependent. It can also grow through your business acumen and affinity for client types such as light manufacturing firms, physician-owned health networks, or car dealerships. Depending on this affinity and your tenure as a financial professional, the relationship between your prospecting and thought leadership will be different.

For newly minted FAs, prospecting and thought leadership are more critical than client service at earlier stages of their development. The successful advisors we work with provide them with the high level of service they expect without losing focus on the need to keep the pipeline full. For the tenured FAs, they're spending more time servicing their ideal clients.

The genesis of *Taming the Four-Headed Dragon* is a product of more than twenty years of personal experience in prospecting for more business on a limited time budget. My firm, ProDirect, provides sales training and coaching to FAs that provides clarity around who's right for their business and structure to their prospecting efforts. We hold clients accountable to what they say they want to achieve within a system that's easy to execute. Clients say they hire me because, not only do I "carry the bag," my messaging and process orientation to client acquisition is intuitive and gets results. The training and coaching I provide adds clarity and importance to the interactions that advisors have with prospects, connections that more often than not lead to a meaningful relationship.

I wrote this book to help you and advisors like you make more money by putting you in position to tell prospects genuinely and authentically why you think they should work with you. In interviewing our clients for the book, they unanimously said their ongoing value from the concepts I will share with you comes from their ability to connect with most any prospect type on the value they deliver. I also wanted to help advisors inject productivity into their practice growth efforts in the face of multiple demands on their time.

The data also shows that advisors want to grow their practices. According to a 2010 survey by SEI, a leading provider of asset management and investment processing solutions, 66 percent of advisors say growing their business is their top priority.

For those new to the business, you can use this book to grow, where more clients truly means more for you. For those advisors looking to break through to their next level of production, you can use this book to help you weed out high-maintenance clients and focus on finding like-minded prospects who value your approach. For those of you with a more transactional book, weighted more heavily in fixed-income solutions, for example, this book may help you move to more sustainable client revenue streams in equities-oriented solutions.

The title of the book, *Taming the Four-Headed Dragon*, represents four core activities or energies facing advisors. The four dragons are as follows:

- **Dragon 1—Clients**. Advisors spend most of their time servicing existing clients in their practice.

- **Dragon 2—Prospects**. For the reasons mentioned previously, most advisors need to prospect for more clients.

- **Dragon 3—Marketing**. Advisors need to network and tell their community about their brand of advisement.

- **Dragon 4—Administration**. From client reviews to required paperwork, advisors need to manage the details of a healthy practice.

The challenge for advisors is that any one of these dragons is competing for your attention at any given time. On its own, each one is important, but based on your tenure and the needs of your clients, these dragons can and most often will require an orchestrated balance.

In your role, you need to manage multiple points of focus—your existing book, a search for new clients, marketing, and compliance and administration. The time demands of these focus areas are draining, and most often, prospecting, the lifeblood of practice growth, suffers in the end. This book will help you beat back these dragons and give you more satisfaction in the client acquisition process.

The job of an FA can be one of the most rewarding in our economy. You get to follow the markets, help people reach their financial and personal goals, and make a decent living while doing it. From my experience, the best advisors really aren't financial professionals at all. They're coaches. They care about people, and like a metal detector on the beach, they're constantly looking for solutions to their clients' problems. If it's not a portfolio strategy, it's a better way to manage the talent in their small business or to figure out how to ascend to a leadership role in their community.

But the recent recession in the global economy and a general skepticism of Wall Street has advisors working harder than ever to grow. While client portfolios have shown signs of growth as we creep into economic recovery, clients are still leery of what lurks around the corner for their investments. Our advisor clients tell us that anything less than 10 percent annualized is a disappointment in their clients' eyes and they all want to outperform the market. They all want high return with low risk.

Commitment from prospects and clients is languishing, and it's not just because of uncertain economic times. Prospects and clients want advice and counsel, but they are not getting it. The door is open for financial professionals to clearly articulate what they want their clients to do and why. Often what I see is more procrastination on the part of clients and prospects because the advisor is not being clear about a concrete next step. From what I see, they don't want to appear too pushy or salesy.

If you add the proliferation of discount brokers and the false notion of safety in the status quo to that, you have a real threat to the growth of the financial advisor model.

Advisors who have moved to a fee-based model have experienced some real gains as the economy has emerged from the recession. But they still need to sign new clients for more-reliable growth and as protection against fluctuating markets. Commission-based advisors also need to grow as they're under pressure to protect account balances while bringing fresh ideas to clients, thoughts that have real dollars associated with them. Even if your practice is a hybrid of both, general market unease and clients' attachment to the status quo makes growth almost mandatory.

As a result, our clients have asked for a system that can get them the growth they need and the type of growth they want with limited time. I wrote *Taming the Four-Headed Dragon* to provide a process to help advisors achieve this growth. My twenty years of experience selling professional services (and coaching those who do the same) has shown that balancing clients, growth, marketing, and administration is doable and a must.

So the *Taming* system helps advisors do four things:

1. It will help you get clear on what you really want. I ask advisors all the time, "Why do you want to grow? Is it because it's the right thing to do? Do you have a goal for your increased income? Can you handle an increased client load?" Without the answers to these questions, most business development activity is reactive, mildly effective, and lacking passion.

2. The system helps get advisors to articulate who is ideal for their practice. The most effective advisors I coach can vividly describe their ideal client relationship, how it looks and how it feels. The best relationships are those based on mutual respect and authenticity, where solutions to client problems are a collaborative effort. Once you know who this is, finding such a client becomes a lot easier.

3. Messaging is next. Routine and effective prospecting happens when you have a great story, one that you and your referral sources love to tell. Typically it captures your actions that have a

special impact, the reason why clients have consciously chosen to work with you, and a reference to why you think you can help a particular prospect. I've included support for creating a value proposition that will resonate with your ideal prospects.

4. The Taming system provides a proven process for interacting with clients and prospects that puts you in position to make an intelligent recommendation. Anyone who is someone worth attracting is smart and successful and has a point of view. Your conversations need to validate these individuals and stimulate dialogue around optional paths forward. My system will help you design conversations that help you help the client choose a best path forward. The high-performing advisors I work with approach these interactions as a thinking partner with prospects to help them make their best decisions.

This four-part system also addresses the need to effectively grow on a limited time budget. Anything our clients do around business development has to work. They don't have time for trial and error.

For the foreseeable future, prospecting time will be challenged with more regulation coming rather than less, so you will have to put dedicated time aside for administration. In addition, those of you who made the move from a wire house to an independent model will have to make up for the lack of big company marketing and create market pull yourself. Just for you, I've added a chapter on marketing your practice.

I've also documented how high-performing advisors develop an ability to know just what time and attention to give each dragon and the process and tools to achieve what good looks like. You'll also find ideas for how to apply the right effort and time against each dragon and adopt the principles in this book in a style that suits you. The book also provides proven tools, messaging, and approaches to help you attract more prospects and close more business. The content I've included is the exact same process I use with my coaching clients and is the only method that I believe can tame the four-headed dragon.

My goal for writing this book was to allow you and your firm to maximize your profit and growth potential, all while achieving a better work/life balance. It's tools-based and easy to read, a must for today's busy FA. By taming the four-headed dragon, our clients have said they've been freed to do their best work.

In the next few chapters, I hope to respect what you know about your profession and what's working. I also hope to provide a window into thinking differently about prospecting and client interaction, thinking that's been shaped not only by a formal graduate education in training but my own experience over the last twenty years selling professional services.

I'll share what works, what prospects and clients respond to, and what the research says as I support my points of view. While that sounds easy and intuitive, this book will provide a proven model for growing your practice in a way that connects you to those who enjoy promoting the positive experience they're having with you. I'll give you tools and language to support interactions that earn you a consistent and positive reputation.

Taming the Four-Headed Dragon will provide you with a practical model that speaks to the real reason you want your practice to grow. I'll leverage what you're already doing well, provide a refreshing look at setting goals, and support you with new and different messaging structures. You'll also find ways to close that will get most any prospect to buy in. I'll share perspectives on connecting with prospects and clients that earn you the right to ask for what you want or, in my language, make an intelligent recommendation.

CHAPTER 1

MEANING MORE TO CLIENTS

I take several approaches when applying my sales techniques to the advisor interaction. Whether it's providing prospecting support, diagnosing client behavior, or strategizing around additional sources of prospects, I apply everything in the ProDirect tool kit. But I always look for one thing that's not in the tool kit when hiring salespeople: the desire to mean more to clients.

Meaning more to clients is about doing what the average advisor doesn't do. It's a belief that anything worth doing is worth overdoing. It's a credo that holds as its highest principle that mediocrity is not an option. And it's an ego drive that pushes you to make yourself indispensable.

For some advisors, this means touting their deep and rich expertise in alternative investments. For others, it's the portfolio construction aspect of separately managed accounts. But the real thrust of meaning more is to be better and different than any other advisor in every respect. The best relationships I've witnessed my clients develop are those where their client asks them for their advice in all things, not just financial. Call it going the extra mile, doing the unexpected, or doing the right thing, it's a mind-set and belief that clients can feel. And most often, this is why you get hired. To grow, your prospecting efforts need to channel your "meaning more to clients" mind-set.

The "Meaning More to Clients" tagline was born over twenty-five years ago when I was working as a sales rep for a global consumer products company. Typically, territories are vacant before another salesperson fills them, and mine had been vacant for over six months. A lot can happen to candy bars and bags of chocolate chips in six months across seventy-five stores, most of it bad. Needless to say, I didn't have a first name for the first three months on the job due to the hundreds of dollars of damaged product left expiring in each store. A common callout was, "Yo, Nestle, your damages are in the back." Knowing I had to be in the job for another sixteen months drove me to find a better way . . . at least to find a way to achieve first-name status.

I wanted badly to be viewed as a trusted resource to my store managers. I didn't want to be seen as just a rep. So I did whatever it took: tracked in and out of stock positions, noted pricing trends, and captured what customers said out of earshot of store employees. I was constantly playing ideas upstream and letting managers know what I did for them that day. Call it winning by a nose, running through the bag, or giving it 110 percent, I did it all. It became a way of being, a way of selling, and later a way of selling strategically to just about any buyer I encountered. I turned myself inside out and became the customer. My customers saw this and felt this.

So when I started my own firm, I wanted to teach people how to do this, that is, how to mean more. I was working with an advisor last year that wanted to mean more to one of his small business prospects. The prospect was the CEO of a $250 million sheet metal fabricator located in the Greater Washington, DC, area. My client had tried everything—logging phone calls, sending serial e-mails, and even faxing the prospect his bio. We had a "meaning more to clients" brainstorming session and came up with a different approach.

We learned that the prospect's son had been named to the starting defense on the West Point football team. Given the geography, we hypothesized that the client would be driving to Bear Mountain every other week in the fall, a five-hour drive. We did some more sleuthing and found that the prospect was a huge Tom Clancy fan. So to mean more, my client sent the prospect a note with four Clancy novels on CD, enclosed with a note congratulating his son and wishing the prospect safe travels with some words from "Tom." The prospect called a week later. The prospect is now a client.

Fig. 1 The Meaning More to Clients Sales Process

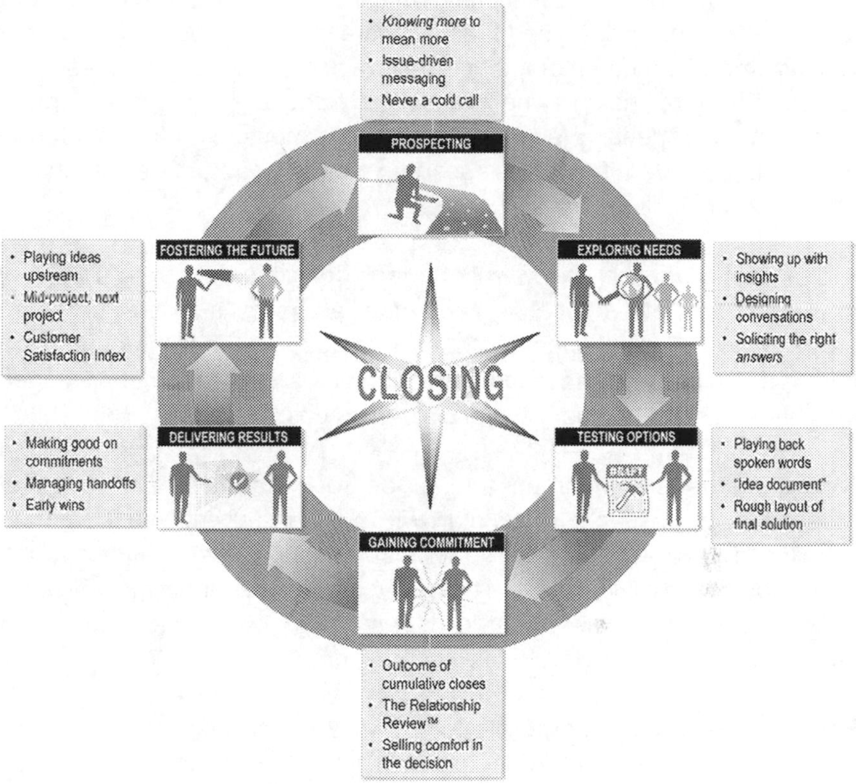

Process for Selling the Way Buyers Buy

As I progressed in my career and now in my own business, meaning more to clients started to take on a life of its own. So I decided I wanted to make it trainable. Many advisors call when they can, send the occasional direct mail piece, and run a prospect dinner with a wholesaler once a quarter. Meaning more is not something that just happens. Rather, it's an intentional process of engaging prospects that validates them across multiple interactions. I actually developed an entire sales model to embody the meaning more mind-set and sell the way clients actually buy.

Prospecting

Prospecting is more than just getting on the phone and dialing away. Your competition does this. In the Meaning More model, prospecting is about knowing more to mean more, that is, leveraging information and research to provide more insight when contacting and engaging a prospect. Successful prospecting leverages client type messaging that particular prospects can identify with, messaging that sounds different than the other advisors calling them.

A dear friend of mine, fellow sales coach John Orvos, says, "The goal in the first part of prospecting [sleuthing, as he calls it] is to come so prepared to the client meeting that you actually have a hypothesis on how you can help. The meeting then becomes an exchange of privileged insights with some mutually beneficial next steps."

"Sleuthing" is a term John and I use to describe the process of researching a prospect. I like to start with his or her client type (corporate exec, small business owner, large physician group practice, and so forth). When you can identify the client type, you can start connecting the issues facing these individuals and start aligning potential solutions at a high level.

For example, retiring corporate execs may or may not have financial planning assistance afforded to them upon their exit and may not have figured out an appropriate rollover vehicle for their assets. Large physician groups leverage economies of scale. One of those economies is profit sharing for its members. Someone on the management team is responsible for this and is typically under pressure to recommend the right solution.

So you might be thinking about how much sleuthing is enough. I like to say that, once you can assess what's changing in this person's environment and what his or her self-interests likely are, you're probably in a good place to conduct a meeting. One of the litmus tests for me is if I feel prepared to be spontaneous in the meeting with a prospect. With an agenda as your compass, you want to feel that, no matter what direction an interaction takes, you're prepared to engage. Once you've done your sleuthing, I recommend sending agendas in advance, asking the prospect to add or subtract to the flow. This starts you on an engagement path early and shows you care about the prospect's time.

Discovery Phase 1: Exploring Needs

This is not about asking a laundry list of clever questions or going deep into a prospect's personal finances. Too many advisors do this in their earnest due diligence, but it comes off as too penetrating too soon. Before asking qualifying types of questions that really benefit you the advisor, you need to earn the right. To do this, it's important to get a feel for what matters most to a prospect. I like to ask my own clients about where they are versus their vision of perfection—with their job, with their finances, or with themselves. Prospects are typically more forthcoming when you pose those types of questions. As part of discovery, be careful to not leave your agenda too open, letting the client dominate the dialogue. It may feel customer-focused, but this can actually work in reverse. Successful, busy prospects expect to be led through a valuable process that's well planned and prospect-focused and promises to add some value at the end. While you don't want to control the person, you can and should control the process. For potential investors, ask about what's not quite right in their current situation. Probe where they might be a little frustrated with what they're not accomplishing and by when. Meaning more in the exploring needs context is less about the questions you ask and more about the questions that help the prospect to self-explore, to hypothesize, and to speculate. In a way, it's more about the answers you want to hear instead of the questions themselves. I've heard many advisors tell me that they had so many questions to ask the prospect that the meeting ended and they weren't able to redirect on any of the answers.

In the discovery process, you also want to validate and affirm the prospect. For example, you want to show respect for what the prospect has already achieved and what he or she has already accomplished with his or her wealth. You also want to pay deference to what he or she already knows about investing. The best advisors we coach actually view this step as an opportunity in conversation to clarify what they're learning and to make sure they've heard the prospect correctly. So think of exploring needs as validating the prospect.

In our experience, less is best when it comes to asking questions of your prospects. In fact, we promote a prospecting dialogue that features three primary questions: priming questions, pebble questions, and payoff questions. The goal of these questions is to get the conversation off to a

5

great start, to uncover issues in the prospect's world, and to start thinking about potential recommendations around how you and your firm can help.

But here is what's different: the primary purpose of initial meetings should not be to educate *you*. It's to establish mutual respect and to get the prospect talking about what matters most to him or her and what he or she wants to accomplish.

In using these questions, you want to get a sense of the relative value of addressing the prospect's issues. All three question types are designed to capture the spoken words of the prospect for your use in communicating your solution later. We all love to feel that we've been heard and understood, and this process will help you accomplish that. So let's look at some of the questions and statements that can help when exploring needs with prospects.

Priming Questions

Priming questions or statements set the tone of the meeting, connect the prospect back to the original purpose of getting together, and jump-start your agenda. Here's a sample priming question:

> *So, Jean, I thought what we could discuss today is your family's need for a financial plan, one that would consider the protection of assets for your retirement as well as the distribution of assets to your heirs. Would that be the right place to start?*

Pebble Questions

Pebble questions uncover a prospect's frustration with a particular financial situation or some constructive discontent around where he or she would like to be with a certain issue.

Pebble questions focus on where the prospect is relative to perfection as he or she sees it. My experience shows that focusing on where a client is relative to his or her ideal situation yields richer insights than focusing on what's wrong. Here is a sample pebble question:

Great, Jean. So let me start by asking where you are relative to what your ideal situation would be for a comprehensive financial plan. Can you share with me some provisions you've been thinking about in advance of today that you'd like to see us include?

OR

So, Jean, it sounds like you've been thinking about a financial plan for your family, particularly as it relates to multigenerational wealth transfer. What would you like to see that some of the other firms you've interviewed are just not addressing?

These pebble questions do a few things:

- They validate that you've been listening.

- It opens the door for Jean in the prior example to tell you what she sees as her ideal situation and what she's not getting.

- These questions prompt the prospect to actually share why and where he or she is dissatisfied so you can gauge next steps and put yourself in position to make what I call an "intelligent recommendation."

Payoff Questions

When payoff questions are asked properly, these questions actually get the prospect to articulate the value of taking action. With payoff questions, you're looking to surface the benefit of doing something about your prospect's problems or issues. Let's look at a few examples:

So, Jean, what I'm hearing you say is that wealth transfer is not the only consideration for choosing a firm to prepare a comprehensive financial plan. You want provisions for family care and certain charitable contributions. If our team could create a plan that would provide you protection and guaranteed execution against all three of your wishes, what level of comfort would that give you that you don't enjoy now?

OR

So, Jean, what if we could deliver all the provisions you are looking for in a financial plan that would provide for systematic wealth transfer, the creation of a trust for your children, and a process for apportioning assets from your estate to the charities you designate? How might you gauge the value of that?

So with payoff questions, you're painting a picture of what you could deliver (based on what you are learning that's relevant to the prospect) and getting the prospect to share the value of taking action. Payoff questions can also act as a more authentic trial close because you're getting the prospect's opinion early on a possible course of action. This is important to protect against prospect procrastination later. These questions typically take place in your first few prospect meetings. What's been helpful for our clients is to actually ask for a separate meeting to present several options after your work in discovery.

Discovery Phase 2: Testing Options

This step acts as a playback of what you've heard from the prospect. This is an important step for three reasons:

1. You want to let the prospect know that you've heard him or her.

2. You want to make sure you've got the facts straight because this is what you will base your intelligent recommendation on.

3. Before you offer a final solution, you want to float your approach first without any fees or executional details.

At this stage, you want to anchor your directional thinking with the prospect by recapping what've you've both discovered thus far. The words I love to hear advisors say to their prospects at this stage are, "Based on what you shared with me, I have a few ideas for you." It's a more credible way to do a trial close, and you're not really closing here. You are looking for the prospect's early opinion. Here's an example:

> *So, Mike, based on what you shared with me, I would recommend an open architecture platform such as National Innovator. It's a sophisticated retirement solution with wide fund choice. We can execute your investing strategies within the products, and the technology makes that easy for us. Can you see the connection to what you were looking for?*

In the previous example, you're reconnecting the prospect to prior stated needs and offering a rationale for your idea. As in all phases of the Meaning More sales process, you want a high level of prospect engagement. It serves no one well by skipping steps or rushing to the close. In my experience, this is the biggest contributor to prospect procrastination and even the loss of a prospect. It's always better to get buy-in now versus later. Plus, if you go to a hard-coded solution too soon, it can be too final for the prospect. Most people want to chew on your recommendation a bit. Some like to talk it out or "use the air as their verbal whiteboard," as I'm fond of saying.

I've also learned that rough layouts often sell better than polished ones. That is, clients buy into what they have a hand in creating. Think of it as a proposal without the money. One of our clients calls it a "proposure," a proposal and brochure all in one.

Often, advisors are too quick to present their solution, especially if they really believe in it. For all the right reasons, most want to appear knowledgeable and ready with an answer. But taking this step actually adds more momentum for a close because you're trading on what the prospect said about his or her problem (literally) and the value of doing something about it. Just be sure that your recommendation is couched in the prospect's spoken words with logical, easy next steps clearly defined.

Gaining Commitment

Done well, the close is a natural consequence of your conversations where all touch points are reviewed and areas of mutual value are expressed. Some call this "the ask," but it's more than that. It's actually your intelligent recommendation supported by the details of your proposal. In those details are the prospect's or client's spoken words, as many as are relevant. The language I love to hear advisors say sounds like this:

> *So, Jean, based on what you shared with us, we've prepared a final proposal that outlines the elements of your financial plan, what happens and when, and when you can expect a finished product. We've also addressed the concerns you had around your retirement and multigenerational wealth transfer with the scenarios you requested. At this time, we have all we need to get started. If there are any other questions or something else to add, please let's discuss that now. Other than that, we have just three items that require your signature, and we can get started. We actually put together a timeline of what happens next, which we should review before you leave today.*

So in the previous example, you're accomplishing a few things:

- You're letting the prospect know that it's proposal time and you've both arrived here because of what you've done *together.*

- You are hinting to concerns that were raised but addressed. This is important because you want to remove any lingering doubts the prospect may have. This sample also shows that you're prepared, not only with the sign-on documents but with a project plan.

At this point, I feel it's important to say that my process is not entirely foolproof. Human behavior can be very dynamic, and prospects do interesting things come commitment time. Plus, it's the prospect's wonderful prerogative to decide when he or she wants to. So your job as the advisor is to paint the picture that taking more time to "think about it" will not add more value to the prospect.

But if you are still experiencing resistance, we recommend a tool called the Relationship Review, which supports a structured conversation that captures what you and the prospect did together and chronicles the journey. I created the tool to decrease the number of meetings required to close a client by reflecting all the value that's been created thus far. The

Relationship Review helps you shape a conversation that recaps all the value that's been exchanged and makes a sign that both parties should be ready to commit.

The Relationship Review Process

1. A brief summary of the relationship (how you got together and how far you've traveled)

2. Meetings held and with whom, lessons learned, and mutual value established

3. Unique needs and options uncovered together

4. Objections raised with satisfactory responses

5. Recommendations

6. Easy next steps for all

Delivery

This is critical for anyone who owns the sale and ongoing relationship. According to Jeff Thull in *The Prime Solution* (2005), the first three weeks after a decision are critical to prove the client made the right decision and the seller captured quick wins. Your clients are no different. They want to feel good about the fact they made the right choice, and you need to start delivering what you promised the client. In fact, at a closing meeting, do your best to create a timeline of what will happen and when for your new client. It's important in the delivery stage. It's also important to check in and let the new client know that things are well in hand and to set the agenda for the next conversation.

Fostering the Future

This is about relationship management done differently. This isn't about random check-ins. Rather, it's an intentional process of follow-up, metrics tracking, and results reviews. We often use the term "midproject, next-project" to frame the best time to offer ideas for additional work with a client. You want to do it when you're midstream with current work that's going well. It's also the perfect time to ask for a referral. Also keep in mind that staying in touch does not always have to be about the client's portfolio. Anything of interest to your client is fair game. Blogs and local business journals are great sources of what's happening so you can keep your client engaged.

I've also found that clients have one of three relationship orientations that advisors should be mindful of over the long haul:

- The Contractual Client is only interested in the facts and nothing but the facts. Forget golf or tickets to a show. He or she wants speed, ease of use, and a high-quality interaction on his or her terms. With these clients, do what you say you are going to do and respond quickly and accurately.

- The Analytical Client can't get enough information. But before you send him or her everything you or your firm has ever written, understand why you are providing the information. Make sure it connects to something relevant for the prospect. Be mindful that most people don't read everything you share with them. So summarize what you send to a client, and use bullet points whenever you can.

- The Collaborative Client values your advice and counsel and will open his or her world up to you so you can best serve him or her. While he or she still expects a high level of service, he or she values and respects your approach and lets you do your job.

So let's go back to the Meaning More to Clients theme. The sales process in figure 1 is really a consulting process, a series of valuable interactions that builds to a mutually beneficial next step. So in your business, what does it look like to mean more? Here's what some of our clients are saying:

Fig. 2 Meaning More Behaviors

✓	doing what you said you were going to do before you said you'd do it
✓	providing unsolicited insights about their business and family
✓	providing books on tape for the commuting client with little time to read
✓	sending invitations to special events or events of interest to the client
✓	providing synthesized analyses, not just data dumps and magazine article cutouts
✓	having consistent interactions in your office by all staff
✓	providing recommendations couched fully in the client's world and his or her spoken words
✓	being asked their opinion
✓	being asked for advice
✓	being asked for coaching
✓	having access to firm leadership and subject-matter experts
✓	providing recognition of any kind
✓	having thoughtful replies to the question "What would you do if you were me?"
✓	having referrals for their business
✓	being intensely listened to

To get the most value from this book, keep this concept of meaning more to clients in mind. As we go through the Taming system, you'll discover points in your relationships where your understanding of prospect-specific issues and challenges merges with your know-how to shape your intelligent recommendations. This system will help you learn how to validate your prospects and get them feeling that they've been heard and understood and that it's time to take action.

Summary

1. Meaning more to clients is about finding ways to add value to prospects and clients as they see it. For some clients, it's about doing what you said you were going to do. For others, it's about providing insights their own staff or family members aren't providing them. It's about going the extra mile as the client defines the distance.

2. Selling to clients must align with how they buy. If you have a client who has done his or her research and knows a lot about your profession, then you need to pay deference to that and ensure that your prospecting process respects that your prospect has done his or her homework. Each step in the Meaning More to Clients sales process has its own distinct purpose and helps you build toward a mutually beneficial outcome (a close). The steps in the meaning more process are prospecting, exploring needs, testing options, gaining commitment, delivering, and fostering the future.

3. Effective prospecting is about knowing whom to call and with what message. While the phone will never go out of style, there are other tools to make contact with a prospect. Your goal is to make a favorable impression over a series of varied and valuable touches that build renown for you and your firm. Your message should align with the client type you are pursuing.

4. Amazon has more than two thousand books for sale that speak to how to ask questions in the sales dialogue. My feeling is that less is more. If you've done your homework, assessed the prospect's client type, and have an intellectual curiosity about him or her, you don't need a laundry list of questions. Rather, the Taming system supports advisors to ask three types of questions. Use a priming question or statement to get meetings off to a great start, a pebble question to assess where the prospect is relative to his or her view of perfection, and a payoff question to get the prospect to articulate the value in removing the pebble.

5. Gaining commitment is closing, but it's more of a culmination of a series of valuable conversations that has brought you both to this point. Often what's missing at this step is a sense of the

total value you've provided thus far in the relationship. Bring the prospect back to the meetings held, value established, objections raised, and resistance addressed.

6. Clients want to feel the value in their decision in the first three weeks. So create a twenty-one-day plan. Isolate quickly the wins you can deliver and reinforce the manner in which you deliver them.

7. Fostering the future is about keeping the idea flow rich with your new client. Share insights valuable to his or her life, business, or family, insights that he or she or his or her own people haven't provided him or her. Introduce him or her to high-value contacts in your network, and deliver on his or her needs for knowledge and education.

CHAPTER 2

TAMING THE FOUR-HEADED DRAGON FOUNDATION

I remember the day I came up with the Taming system. A prospect of mine had asked to see me in action before committing to more serious discussions about working together. So I pulled together a theme and an invite. (I called it a Growth Strategies Workshop for Financial Professionals.) I wanted to put on a good show, but I also wanted to add value to all the attendees. We had an assortment of advisors, planners, and private client advisors attending who were all curious about how they could grow their business. With only a two-hour agenda, I thought about what the takeaways should be.

Everyone needs more prospects and an easier way to land them, so I started there. But then I came back to the obstacles that stand in the way of prospecting ease for my advisor coaching clients. Most say they don't have time to be strategic with their business development. "I'm too busy with admin and internal meetings" is a common reply. But I wasn't hearing the goals these advisors had set for themselves. It seemed everyone was driven by the metrics that their firm was setting for them. I know from my own experience that execution without inspiration is going through the motions with a different mask. So the first Taming inspiration was a goal-setting module.

As I prepped for this growth strategies session at my club, I also thought about the ideal clients of the folks coming to the event. So I reached out to a few local advisors and asked them who's ideal. After the sarcastic "anyone with $2 million to invest," I heard the common themes of retirement planning and generic portfolio management. I didn't hear a crisp codification of the type of client that was ideal for these advisors. Investable assets can never tell you what prospects need or why they might consider leaving their current FA. What will help you, however, is understanding the source of their wealth and the way they currently interact with it. So I added a client profiling mini module to the session.

I also tested the messaging my clients were using for their centers of influence. Every one of them felt confident in his or her pitch until I asked each to speak the words. Without going into the gory details, it all sounded vanilla and unrehearsed. I firmly believe that an advisor's messaging is his or her most valuable yet inexpensive asset he or she possesses. The quality of an advisor's messaging is directly proportionate to the success he or she has in prospecting. The best messaging resonates with a prospect when he or she hears alignment with what he or she needs, combined with the impact the FA has had on the lives of his or her clients. So the Taming system features a messaging clinic.

The quality of an advisor's messaging is directly proportionate to the success he or she has in prospecting.

But I wanted to put one more piece into the talk. I realized that, when these financial professionals left my session, at some point, they would *speak* to someone. So I added a conversation component that is now a feature of the Taming system.

So that's the foundation of the Taming the Four-Headed Dragon system. Let's go into more detail about each part of the model.

Fig. 3 Taming the Four-Headed Dragon (The Model)

Taming the Four-Headed Dragon Model

Goal Setting: Creating the Pull

The goal-setting piece of the model used to be pretty regimented, but I've walked back from that approach in recent years. I take a whatever-it-takes method to setting goals. I believe any activity related to setting goals is good activity. My experience shows that most people will fall off track from a structured goal-setting program. This is significant because most businesspeople are hard on themselves, so falling off track from setting goals can start to feel punitive. Many start to associate negative feelings toward setting goals as momentum wanes. Because most of us tend to avoid pain and seek pleasure, most structured goal-setting programs fail to reach their intended outcome.

I've found that there are two types of goal setters: planners and visionaries.

Planners

Planners need the workbook, the CDs, and their tasks set in an e-mail application with concrete follow-ups and to-dos. Planners purchase noted programs with seminars, CDs, companion workbooks, or digital planning tools with tasks and to-dos. But most of the advisors I work with never complete these programs.

It's probably because these advisors are one of the other types of goal setters out there, the visionary. By visionary, I don't mean a pie-in-the-sky brainstormer with delusions of grandeur. Rather, visionaries connect visually to an end state, some definite expectation for themselves that they can describe. The high-performing advisors I work with can define what success looks like and have an expectation that they'll get there.

Visionaries

Visionaries take a view of a definite future and set goals that create a pull, objectives that have meaning and excite them. Many refer to this pull as the law of attraction, the universal law that responds to your every thought, negative or positive, that will always bring you what you think about most.

Visionaries see value in scheduled events and tasks for setting goals, but what's more important to them is the right goal and the right path.

Profiling the Ideal Client

In my coaching work around setting goals, I've realized that most advisors look at prospects too generically. My experience shows that, with a little introspection and research, you can come up with a sketch view of what an ideal prospect would look, sound, and feel like. So I set out to create some diagnostic tools to select the right criteria of ideal and to rank prospects against them.

Some of the criteria that advisors tell me are working well for them include:

- assets over $2 million

- assets over $5 million

- prior success with this type of prospect

- comfort with the complexity of alternative investments

- growth opportunity for a managed money platform

- likability

- interest in my firm's diagnostic tools

- prospect needs aligned with the solutions I can offer

- open reception to education and professional growth

- solution-focused compared to transaction-focused

- in alignment with how I want to do business

- respect for my process

- a client type I understand and find deep interest in (for example, large physician groups)

Part of ideal client identification is uncovering a prospect's willingness to change. Anyone worth working with is probably with another advisor.

So most often, the sales process for advisors is about change and conversion. That means your business development efforts need to align with that. In fact, my coaching assignments over the last decade have revealed this as the number-one source of procrastination among prospects. Sales opportunities are breaking down because there's not enough of a burning platform for them to change. So I went to school on how I could help advisors codify the change appetite of prospects and then interact with them accordingly.

To help advisors best calibrate their approach with prospects and clients, I came up with the behaviors of five typical change types in the advisor-prospect relationship:

1. They are eager to change but are highly inquisitive and prepared. They are willing to recommend but are reserved. They are the strong, silent type.

2. They jump at the chance to refer. They are early adopters of ideas and new processes. They love kickoffs and special events.

3. They are willing to change with good reason. This type can't get enough research and data.

4. They have a follow-the-herd mentality. Only when the benefits are boldly obvious will they change.

5. They abhor change to the point that they will take you off track, challenge your assumptions, and derail your argument.

The idea of the Taming approach is to identify and spend more time with the clients who are most ideal and most likely to change. Each one of these types requires its own individual approach and presents an opportunity for you. While some avoid those adverse to change at all costs, some take them on for sport. My feeling is that you need to cultivate early adopters and brace for the effort needed to convert the skeptics.

Messaging

The third part of the Taming model is messaging. From my research back in 2010, I found that two things were hamstringing advisors as they related to their prospecting:

- I'm not confident in my story.

- I'm not really sure who I should be calling on.

So I tried to reverse-engineer that paradigm to focus on crisp messaging for both prospects and referral sources. Best practice shows that the best messaging conveys three important things:

1. Who you are, where you're from, and why that's special

2. Why other clients consciously choose to work with you

3. Why you thought this prospect would be interested in learning more

Part one is pretty intuitive, but parts two and three deserve a little explanation because this is where your success in prospecting will lie. Part two is really the credibility step in messaging. It's important to convey to prospects what you do (your brand of advisement) and why others choose to work with you. If you don't know this, please put this book down right now and call your best clients and ask them. You need this insight because this is what you will trade on. This part drives credibility for you and begins to create a picture for the prospect of what it would be like to work with you.

Part three is where your message hits home for the prospect. My clients often hear me say, "Everyone wants to hear his or her name in lights." (Note the play on words.) It also reflects what you know about prospects of this type. The capstone of your messaging should always reflect that you've researched your prospect and have a few early ideas on how you might be able to help. Push yourself to arrive at a hypothesis on what solutions might be right for this prospect. This should be your goal.

Part three, or your "you" statement, is where you acknowledge what prospects like them are typically frustrated with, energized by, or motivated about. According to John Orvos, the author of *The Four Faces of Sales*, this part also speaks to the problems associated with their client type and your unique ability to help. The goal is to get the prospect to sense that you're fluent in the issues associated with his or her situation.

One of the client types I often see are newly married couples commingling finances for the first time. Often they both have multiple 401(k)s from previous employers, typically with similar holdings.

Closing

As part of our 2010 research, we also looked at closing as a real issue for advisors. In surveying division and branch managers, we found that less than 30 percent of advisors were closing prospects on an outcome. Said another way, too many advisors were letting the prospect control the sales process versus being more assertive by recommending a pathway themselves. Likely fearing rejection as a setback in the relationship, too much emphasis was placed on pleasantries and value-adds. This was likely a product of the relationship orientation in asset management distribution at the time. We all lost sight of asking for what we believed would be a valuable next step for fear of being too pushy or salesy.

So I set out to create a closing program that would blend effective language with an intuitive conversation process. We borrowed from the pharmaceutical industry, where reps have ninety seconds or less to make a relevant connection with a physician. I found that, in certain environments, such as tumor board presentations and case reviews, reps could actually have deeper discussions if they focused less on their product and more on a patient type. At the time, I thought advisors could do the same but, in your case, focus on a client investor type. I also added a problem element. Discerning investors want to talk about their situations and are interested in how you can help if you've surfaced an understanding of their problems the right way. Keep in mind that, when I use the word "problem," I mean some level of dissatisfaction with where an investor is against his or her view of perfection or expectation.

As a result of this experience, I created a closing framework to foster better dialogues relevant to prospects' situations. I call it CPS, or Client Type-Problem-Solution. By engaging in an investor-based conversation grounded in who they are and surfacing problems or dissatisfaction with their current situation, you create an opening for an eventual solution recommendation because there's context in the dialogue. The benefit to CPS is that it takes advantage of all the sleuthing you've done and puts it into a workable discussion format.

Think about the last time you went to the doctor for a sore throat. Did you get the script for antibiotics on the way in or the way out? Thus, successful advisors are shaping effective closing conversations framed in a CPS format.

Successful advisors shape effective closing conversations framed in a CPS format.

CPS also works to slow advisors down in conversation. It's so easy to launch into firm accolades or success stories, especially if you're proud of them. But wealthy investors don't want a pitch. They've heard them all before. Rather, they want a trusted resource that understands their client type and all the nuances that go with it. Once a prospect feels you understand his or her unique situation, he or she tends to be more responsive to recommendations. Client types typically have sets of recognizable characteristics. These characteristics line up with a certain set of problems your solutions are uniquely capable of supporting.

You might already be working with the following client types: newly married professional couple, physician-owned medical group, CEO of a light manufacturing firm, recently retired senior executive, wealthy family looking for generational wealth solutions, or owner of a multilocation oil and lube franchise. Each one of these client types, as a product of his or her client type, has certain problems or dissatisfaction in his or her financial world. The CPS process helps you address some of the typical questions on the minds of such prospects:

- Why should I work with you? Why do you want to work with me?

- What do you know (or have the capacity to know) about my unique situation?

- Are you going to pitch me on the flavor of the month?

- Will I have options?

- I'm already working with someone. Why should I change?

Following this framework also keeps you from rushing in too soon to offer a recommendation. Think about it. Do you want the salesperson at Best Buy recommending a fifty-five-inch 3D flat screen with a floor stand in your six-hundred-square-foot New York City apartment? Probably not. But you may be looking to enhance your viewing experience with a flat-screen TV with the ability to store components out of sight given the configuration of your living room that doubles as your bedroom. A good salesperson would uncover that and make a recommendation only when the real problem is surfaced.

I'm also seeing a hangover from the relationship push in asset management over the last ten years. While innocent in its intent, this orientation left financial professionals with don't-push-too-hard-or-you'll-damage-the-relationship thinking. This notion quashed strategic thinking and a reluctance to suggest mutually beneficial next action. I feel that, if you're not free to be curious and if you can't recommend ideas, you really don't have a relationship.

Higher levels of sophistication in portfolio construction and a wider array of asset management products available have also lengthened the sales process for most advisors. With more moving parts and the need for incremental prospect understanding, many sales opportunities are stalling. Prospects are often losing track of where they are in the sales process and the value that the advisor has created over time. While we as salespeople always recollect more about the meetings we've had, what was said, and what the logical next step is in the sales process, prospects really have no idea.

In the case of these more complex sales as with separately managed accounts, nonqualified executive benefit plans, or midmarket retirement plans, often the best value an advisor can provide is letting the prospect know where he or she is and the tangible value of taking the next step.

In chapter 9, we'll talk about the Relationship Review, a tool designed to get stalled sales situations unstuck. (See figure 4.) Advisors have a major opportunity to let prospects know how they got started together, the mutual value they've established, and the responses to any and all resistance thus far in the process.

Fig. 4 The Relationship Review Tool

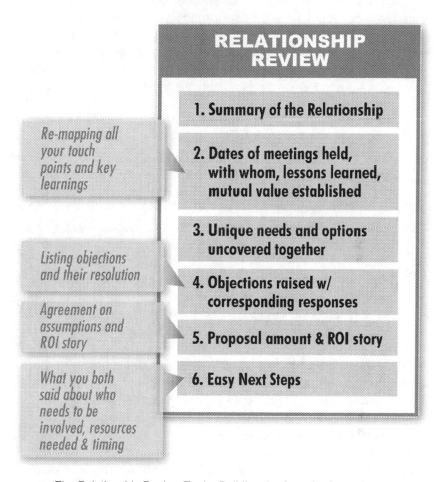

The Relationship Review Tool—Building the Case for Commitment

The rationale for the tool is to give everyone involved the comfort that the advisor/prospect team has left no stone unturned. For advisors, the intention is to get the prospect to realize that he or she needs to make a decision. As I tell all of my clients, at this step of the sales process, you'd rather have a no than a maybe. You can't put maybes on a pipeline.

Summary

1. Taming the four-headed dragon is about managing the competing energies of client management, prospecting, thought leadership, and administration. What often gets short shrift is prospecting, the lifeblood of growing your practice as an advisor. Taming the four-headed dragon effectively requires four things: proper goal setting, ideal client identification, crisp messaging, and effective conversation management. One dragon without the others is just activity. Remember, you only have a fraction of your time for prospecting. It has to be amazing.

2. Most ideal clients are working with another advisor. Therefore, your sales process is all about change. We have identified five change types that you are likely to encounter that require their own unique interaction strategy.

3. Your best clients will come from referral, so you need to equip your referral base with great messaging.

4. The best messaging includes who you are and why that is special, what you do and why other clients consciously choose to do it with you, and why you thought the prospect would be interested in learning more.

5. A lack of closing success comes from rushing too soon to offer a solution. Often what is needed are dialogues that validate a specific client type, work/life issues associated with that type, and a select few solutions to those issues. That is how people buy; thus, it is how you should sell.

6. You should utilize a process for closing that brings the prospect back to how you met, the mutual value that was established, your recommendations, the way you resolved any resistance, and the next steps.

7. You should ensure that prospects are aware of all the value you've added to them in the sales process.

CHAPTER 3

TAMING SYSTEM STEP 1:
SETTING THE RIGHT GOALS

I always wonder how I've accomplished all I have. I don't keep a journal regularly. I've purchased and skimmed three books on setting goals and own probably every business productivity tool ever marketed. Yet I seem to be doing okay. But like you, I'd like to be more than okay. So I've tried to find the best thinking on setting goals. In my ongoing study of successful people, I also find that successful people think thoughts of abundance and wealth and don't let negative thinking or critics interrupt their expectations around their goal.

The following are some goal-setting best practices of the high-performing advisors we work with:

1. Have a clearly defined goal. The goal is something you are emotionally connected to, something you want very much.

2. Have a clearly established plan that you work regularly.

3. Have the courage to adjust your plan and expectations as circumstances arise.

4. Reject any and all negativity from friends, colleagues, or relatives, and block out any reference that the goal cannot be accomplished.

5. Establish a mastermind group of two or more people who encourage, support, and assist wherever possible.

The key to setting goals, the kind that gets results, is getting really clear on what you want. High-performing advisors visualize a goal that they're viscerally connected to, and they don't let anyone's negativity take them off track. They get together with people they trust, people who will hold them accountable. I actually did this before I started my company, ProDirect, and the response was overwhelming. Ask for coaching and advice. You'll have many takers.

As a student of success, I've realized that some of the most successful people haven't used a Franklin Planner and have never been to a Tony Robbins seminar. What they have in common, though, is a vision and a clear understanding of why they want to accomplish a goal. These same successful people also possess a very specific expectation of success connected to their vision. What I believe gets lost for advisors in goal-setting tools and planners is the fact that many don't have a concrete expectation of a definite result. So that's why I coach advisors to be creative, to think big with a reason. I would never want anyone to feel that it's punitive or remedial. If you feel that setting goals is a task, then setting goals becomes just that, a tedious process. There is enough process in our businesses and our lives right now.

It's very easy to go into setting goals with guns blazing only to fall off pace due to travel or some combination of other commitments. Because most successful people are pretty competitive, I see advisors blaming themselves for falling off track. This attracts even more negativity to setting goals and often keeps advisors from doing it altogether. So why fall into this trap?

Goal setting is a visual phenomenon, period. What happens when we set a goal in motion visually is that we set a certain vibration in motion, one that manifests itself in more material ways as you sharpen your focus on it. A good friend of the firm and executive coach John Miller is fond of saying, "What you focus on grows."

What you focus on grows.

The Vision Board

So based on my experience in helping advisors get what they want, combined with some of the irrefutable tenets of the law of attraction, I recommend that advisors articulate their goals visually on what I call a vision board.

Actually, it doesn't need to be a board at all. Just create some separate media that holds the images of what you want to accomplish that is visible to you most of the time. Your vision board will help cement what is important to you and why. A vision board is simply a visual representation or collage of the things you want to have, be, or do in your life. The best ones we've seen our clients create consist of sturdy cardstock or poster board with cutout pictures, drawings, and/or writing that represent the things they want in their lives or the things they want to become. The purpose of the vision board is to activate the law of attraction to begin to pull things from your external environment that will enable you to realize the goals you have determined as important.

By selecting pictures and words that charge your emotions with feelings of passion and excitement, you'll begin to manifest those things into your practice. Best of all, it works. I tell this to participants at all my seminars. It typically sounds like this: "The club you're sitting in, the watch on my wrist, and the conversation we are all having were all on my vision board." Once in a while, I throw in the story of the drum set I had on my vision board, the one that now sits gathering dust in my daughter's playroom. It looks good sitting there though!

My vision board is actually very crude. It's a letter-sized sheet of paper that hangs off a shelf in my office in clear eyeshot. I draw on it, paste cutout pictures to it, and often clip other references to my goals to it. I recommend eight to ten entries. If there's too many, you'll lose your focus. But it has to be in your line of sight. For those of you in an office setting, clip it to the side of your PC monitor just out of eyesight of your colleagues and clients.

Fig. 5 Vision Board

Vision Board Sample

Here are some general guidelines for a well-designed vision board:[1]

Visual

Your subconscious mind works in pictures and images, so make your vision board as visual as possible with images that directly reflect what you want. You can supplement your pictures with words and phrases to increase the emotional response you get from it.

---

[1] Vision board guidelines compliments of Tristan Loo, leading authority on human potential and personal effectiveness.

Emotional

Each picture on your vision board should evoke a positive emotional response from you. The mere sight of your vision board should make you happy and fuel your passion to achieve it every time you look at it.

Strategically Placed

Your vision board should be strategically placed in a location that gives you maximum exposure to it. You need to constantly bathe your subconscious mind with its energy in order to manifest your desires quicker.

Personal

This is your creation of what you want. If you fear criticism or justification of your vision board from others, then place it in a private location so only you can see it.

When creating your vision board, you must do more than just paste a clip of an Audi. It has to be a black on tan Audi R8 or silver A8L, for example. For your house on Cannon Beach in Portland, Oregon, it needs to reflect the color, the type of shingles, the smell in the air, and the type of fireplace. Throw in how you think you'll feel when you're in it. For the desire to speak Italian fluently, include the first town you'll visit to show off your new skill. Get the picture?

For advisors, this can't be about more money or more clients. It's more about why you want more money or more clients. Start with the why. Is it because:

- I want to feel great because I not only created a practice but I am growing it through referral. I want that feeling that comes from so many people hearing about me and benefitting from my process.

- I want more money because I eventually want to run my practice from a sixty-foot Hatteras and be able to spend more time with my wife.

- I want more clients because that way I can grow, get more office space, and eventually turn my business over to an operating partner. That way, I can spend more time facilitating pet adoptions, my real passion.

- I want more money because now I can afford the $2,000 in tires I need each weekend to race my vintage 911.

- I want more money because I can then take the entire extended family on vacation to Tuscany, including airfare.

In setting goals, we always need the because. So let me ask you to plot five items that might be candidates for your vision board. Be clear on why you want to achieve each one.

Fig. 6 Goal Setting: Charting the Reasons Why

Visual Goal 1:		Because:	
Visual Goal 2:		Because:	
Visual Goal 3:		Because:	
Visual Goal 4:		Because:	
Visual Goal 5:		Because:	

Sample:

Visual Goal 1: Own a seven-bedroom house in Sea Girt, Ocean Drive, with brown siding

Because: *I can live there year-round and never need a summer house.*

Visual Goal 2: Buy a five-piece Pearl drum set

Because: I want the feeling of playing "The Ocean" by Led Zeppelin, the live version.

Visual Goal 3: Take a vacation with extended family to Tuscany (Castellina) with pool and bicycles

Because: Tuscany holds something for everyone, as well as many walkable towns.

Visual Goal 4: Achieve board member status by the next election for my favorite charitable cause

Because: I can have more control over how we raise money for research.

Visual Goal 5: Spend two hours of uninterrupted time with my family each night

Because: It enriches me and gives me an opportunity to share and give and to try out my new jokes (even the ones that bomb).

One of my clients has worked a vision board to his advantage. On the board, he placed a beachfront home on the New Jersey Shore, a vintage Porsche Carrera, and a membership to a local country club. While the beachfront house is still a work in process, this client now possesses everything else on that first vision board and has reloaded it three times in the last two years.

Whatever it takes to complete your vision board is fair game. Keeping it fun, purposeful, and relevant keeps setting goals from feeling punitive or administrative. Keeping it fun helps you accomplish more, and that's always a good thing.

Now for you planners, here is a mind-set and a few tools for how to be more successful in your approach to setting goals. Let me just start with a few tenets, and we can go from there.

1. Use a system that works for you and limits the moving parts. For Outlook users, get synched up with Google Calendar so you can

pick up your tasks and compelling events no matter the device or location.

2. Understand that you will get interrupted. You will have a trip, a change in priorities, or a period of free-flowing thought and action, otherwise known as a funk. But don't fear funks. You are human. We all fall into funks. Just know that funks are just the way that our mind and body recharge for something big, something exciting. Often it just takes some support and positive energy to get us back on track. The key is to not beat yourself up if you fall off track or miss one of your targets in setting goals.

Please don't beat yourself up if you fall off track or miss one of your targets in setting goals.

The most successful people I know are constantly reevaluating and recalibrating what they want to accomplish. Challenge yourself, but reward small accomplishments. And by all means, celebrate small wins. Treat yourself to something good like a massage, a new pair of shoes, or those tennis lessons you've been meaning to commit to.

Here are a few tools to help planners in their goal attainment. For planners and folks who like process, we've found it helpful to start with an absolute result, something you're totally committed to at its highest level.

Next, set an absolute result for the coming year, something you're totally committed to, and put a number to it. For example, increase net new prospects by 20 percent, grow your team to five advisors, and so forth. Break your number-one absolute result into thirty-day increments. Once you've done that, enter a list of supporting goals (and purpose) for each thirty-day period to help attain your absolute result. Articulate your vision of the result and outcome. Be specific!

Take a look at the tool in figure 7. In this example, we break out some purposeful activity to support an absolute result. You'll see thirty-, sixty-, and ninety-day breakouts of supporting goals that will help this advisor get to where he wants to be.

Fig. 7 30/60/90-Day Goal-Setting Tool

**My #1 Absolute Result for 2013: Growing My
Newly Converted Prospects by 20 Percent**

By When	Supporting Goals	Purpose	1–30 Days Results/Outcome
7/31	1. Create my ideal client profile. 2. Draft an elevator pitch and test with trusted peers. 3. Chart seven-touch strategy for ten high-value prospects.	To get clear on who is right for me and what messaging will resonate	I will create a validated ideal client profile with messaging that I feel comfortable communicating to a list of potential prospects.

By When	Supporting Goals	Purpose	31–60 Days Results/Outcome
10/31	1. Put three pieces of mail out to three new prospects daily. 2. Make eleven calls by 11:00 a.m. daily. 3. Create the perfect leave-behind.	To make valuable contact with prospects and referral sources	Assuming a 25 percent conversion rate, I will have contacted forty new qualified prospects each month.

By When	Supporting Goals	Purpose	61–90 Days Results/Outcome
1/31	Create webinar on my firm's alternative investments. 1. Construct mailing on ETFs. 2. Revisit seven-touch strategy for ten high-value prospects.	To ensure market message and scheduled contacts are consistent with what ideal clients are seeking and/ or responding to	I will have a more qualified pipeline of prospects with real incentives to meet and a platform for discussions about solutions to client type problems.

As a best practice, complete this goal planner, and keep it visible. I like using a plastic document protector, one that lets you look at a document at a glance while protecting it from getting trashed in your briefcase. I use a clear plastic clamp binder from Staples.

Nix the Lengthy To-Do List

To help you reach your thirty-, sixty-, and ninety-day goals, do not make a lengthy to-do list. Long lists just create more anxiety around what you're not getting done. High-performing advisors get a lot done because they're realistic with what they're capable of doing with the time they have available. I coach clients not to do a big master list for several reasons.

1. You want to minimize the chance that you'll fall off the detail wagon of your goal setting. Goal setting needs to be fluid so you can adjust as events and priorities change.

2. If you box yourself into tight time frames and too many tasks, you'll start beating yourself up as soon as you fail to complete them.

High-performing advisors are realistic with what they're capable of doing with the time they have available.

Experience tells me that successful advisors can realistically get six major things done in a day. So what are the top six things you need to get done today? I recommend that advisors utilize a daily worksheet like this one:

Fig. 8 Daily Success Worksheet: The Big Six Tool

Daily Success Worksheet	
Today's High-Level Focus: The Four-Headed Dragon	
1. Clients	3. Thought Leadership
2. Prospects	4. Admin

My Daily Big Six	
ITEM	**IMPACT**
1.	
2.	
3.	
4.	
5.	
6.	
Notes:	

Daily Success Worksheet: Sample	
Today's High-Level Focus: The Four-Headed Dragon	
1. Clients: the Jensens, Lojolla Medical, Klemp Tool & Die	3. Thought Leadership: This week's blog post, networking at the Union League, postcards for wellness message
2. Prospects: Tingle Partners, John Rauch, Sherman Medical	4. Admin: Learn new CRM system; check on confirmation suppression issue, quarterly updates for Zipper Inc. and the Roberts Family; performance reviews

My Daily Big Six	
ITEM	**IMPACT**
1. 11 x 11 Rule: see CRM system	Hit goal of forty new prospects for the month.
2. 3 x 3 Rule	Get new financial wellness message out to the marketplace to cement firm's differentiation brochure and postcard.
3. Finalize presentation to Sherman Medical Group, and get buy-in from product team.	Have accurate and complete presentation to help senior partner align group around 401(k) and profit-sharing plan.
4. Meet with Klemp Tool and Die CEO to confirm exit plan and involvement in valuation process.	Have goal to get the go sign to invest half the proceeds from the sale of the company.
5. Performance review for two junior associates.	Get them ready for roles in production.
6. Send Tom Clancy novel (Kindle version) to Dirk Bollester.	Son is starting CB on West Point football team. Will have long drives from VA. Dirk wants to convert his firm's DB plan.
NOTES: Spend time learning Growth Outlook tool today; need for Melendez family plan.	

Now that you have an idea of how to use the Big Six tool, you now need to finesse the four dragons. Based on the evolution of your practice and your tenure as an FA, you will have a different emphasis on prospecting, client work, and thought leadership.

Summary

1. Setting goals should not be punitive. If it is, you're not focused on the right goals.

2. Setting goals is control.

3. You should set an absolute result for the coming year, something you're totally committed to, and put a number to it. You should tell your mastermind group about it. They will hold you accountable.

4. There are two types of goal setters: visionaries and planners. Visionaries typically accomplish more.

5. In setting goals, you should get clear on what you want. If you can't articulate it, you should draw it.

6. Setting goals is a visual experience that fosters an expectation of what you want. You can't achieve exactly what you really want unless it is manifested in its visual form.

7. Using a vision board for goal setting represents goals that you are excited about and can put a reason why behind their achievement.

8. Most advisors have unrealistic expectations of what they can accomplish in a day.

9. You should nix the long to-do list. It's an invitation for disappointment.

10. ProDirect research shows that it's reasonable to chart six big accomplishments for any day and the impact they have on each of your four dragons.

CHAPTER 4

DRAGON AND TIME MANAGEMENT: IMPORTANT VS. URGENT

As of this writing, there are over 113,000 books for sales on Amazon. com on time management. What does that tell you? Other than maybe it's time to write your own time management book, it tells me that no one has cracked the code. The reasons are many, but a few ring out for me. Time has different dimensions for all of us. Some of us live in fifteen-minute intervals. Some wait for Friday afternoon to make weekend plans. Some of us see leverage in time, while some see time getting in the way of a path to a better place. No matter what your view, it's important to realize that it's truly an advisor's most precious commodity. Time has growth and client retention implications.

For those building a practice, the time spent on prospecting is directly impacting your revenue. It's important to understand how you *use* time. Can you go the distance and work in a focused manner all day long? Or are you an intensity versus duration person who can outwork anyone in short bursts of activity? Which are you?

To make sure you're leveraging your time to achieve optimal growth in your practice, it's important to know just what activities take up your time. An effective way to do this is singling out what is urgent versus what is important. I've found that the lack of clarity between the two is sapping advisor productivity.

> **For those building a practice, the time spent on prospecting is directly impacting your revenue.**

It was said that General Dwight D. Eisenhower was a master time and task manager. Eisenhower's quote, "What is important is seldom urgent and what is urgent is seldom important," was the late Steven Covey's inspiration to create the Urgent/Important Matrix to help us all focus on activities that make us the most effective.

The Urgent/Important Matrix is a powerful way of thinking about priorities. Using it helps you overcome the natural tendency to focus on urgent activities so you can clear enough time to focus on what's really important. This is the way you move from firefighting into a position where you can work on your practice rather than working in it. So let's look at the definition of what's important versus what is urgent.

- **Important** activities have outcomes that lead to the achievement of your goals.

- **Urgent** activities demand immediate attention. The consequences of not dealing with them are immediate.

Another way to look at urgent and important is this. Urgent activities help you maintain value; these activities keep all aspects of your practice functioning and moving forward. Important activities are those that create value; these strategic imperatives and objectives are compelling and take your practice to greater heights. This isn't an either-or proposition. For advisors, it's important to balance both and understand where they fit.

Fig. 9 Important vs. Urgent Matrix

	Urgent	Not Urgent
Important	• client or market crises • portfolio review meetings • deadline-driven projects • short-term goals	• preparation • new website • relationship building • long-term practice planning

Not Important • interruptions (e-mail, phone, drop-bys, etc.) • some meetings • some requests from others	• trivial busywork • some socializing • personal e-mails • personal Facebook visits

So let's work around the matrix. We've plotted some of the activities that are representative of the levels of urgency and importance in each. Hint: The bottom two boxes are where most advisors lose most of their productivity!

Urgent and Important (upper left box)

There are two distinct types of urgent and important activities that advisors come across: ones that you could not see coming and others that got left to the last minute. These are also tasks that help you maintain the value you are delivering in your practice.

Not Urgent but Important (upper right box)

These are the strategic activities that help you achieve the goals on your vision board and complete important work. High-performing advisors make sure they have plenty of time to do these things properly so they do not become urgent. These activities actually enhance the value you are providing in your practice.

Urgent and Not Important (lower left box)

Urgent but not important activities stop you from achieving your goals and prevent you from completing your work. But these activities often wear a cloak of importance. A common source of these time busters is interruptions from others in your office. Try setting times when you're available so people only interrupt you at certain times. Think open calendar versus open door.

Not Urgent and Not Important (lower right box)

These activities are just a distraction and should be avoided. Some can simply be ignored. Others are activities that other people may want you to do, but they do not contribute to your own goals and priorities.

Looking back to the four dragons, here is how you should view urgent versus important to maximize your productivity and create optimal time leverage:

Fig. 10 Urgent and Important Activities and the Four-Headed Dragon

In this example, take a look at the connection to the time aspects of each dragon for a budding advisor. You'll see that, for this FA, his or her urgency is prospecting with more strategic time allotted for client development. These FAs need to watch that administration and new clients don't monopolize their prospecting time because asset accumulation is their priority at this stage.

Dragon 1—Clients	**Important, not Urgent**
Dragon 2—Prospecting	**Important and Urgent**
Dragon 3—Thought Leadership	**Important, not Urgent**
Dragon 4—Administration	**Not Important and Urgent**

So where do you spend your time (assuming a fifty-hour workweek)?

Dragon	Hours per Week
Clients	
Prospecting	
Thought Leadership	
Administration	

In my experience, here is how we see productive advisors using their time and managing their dragons. Thought leadership (your point of view, networking, and marketing) takes on different meaning as the practice evolves. In addition, time pours back into existing clients as relationships become more prolific and operate as the dominant source of new business. Administration grows later on, given the volume of more clients. Let's take a look at some ideal time splits for FAs new to the business versus more seasoned advisors.

Fig. 11 Ideal Time Splits to Tame the Four-Headed Dragon

Ideal Time Splits (New Advisor)

- clients: 20%

- prospecting: 60%

- thought leadership: 15% info gathering, networking, and social media

- admin: 5%

Ideal Time Splits (Seasoned Advisor)

- clients: 40%

- prospecting: 30%

- thought leadership: 20% research, writing, publishing, and networking

- admin: 10% (more clients = more time, but supported by process)

Admin should always be less than 10 percent and never addressed during prime time.

Here are some success factors I've gleaned from my work coaching advisors, helping them to be the most productive in balancing important and urgent activities:

- The 11 x 11 Rule: Place eleven calls by 11:00 a.m. These can be prospects or clients. The key is to place calls that are closest to the money first. What proposals are outstanding? Address those issues first. In addition, you should be calling at least five existing clients daily to touch base and let them know you are thinking about them. You can use this call to ask if they have any concerns, to remind them that they have a review meeting coming up, or to find out what is going on in their life.

- The 3 x 3 Rule: Set three appointments per day and send three thought pieces to specific prospects daily. These pieces can also satisfy various touches in a drip-type contact plan. Get a sense for what the average postage is for your best pieces, and have that ready in advance. Stamps.com is a great way to do that with a few keystrokes of your computer. This way, no matter where you are, you can drop something in the mail.

- The Power Hour: The Power Hour is about focus. Research suggests that the average executive in corporate America has only seventeen minutes of uninterrupted time per hour. For advisors, it's pretty close to that as well. Given this dynamic, set a specific time of day to make your calls, and let others know you're doing it. Make the calls that are "closest to money" first and then connect with prospects with the greatest affinity next. But do this at a time when you're at your best. Let people know when you're in your power hour, and have them respect that boundary. When thinking about the best time for your power hour, when will your prospects be available? Typically, first thing in the morning, right before lunch, right after lunch, and after most of the workforce has gone home are ideal times. If you don't know the prospect well, avoid calling him or her at home in your early prospecting efforts. I like advisors to earn the right to do that first.

- Create Movement: Business development is a kinesthetic activity. Get your body in motion, connect with people, and make your calls standing up. Invest in a really good headset. Breathe.

Summary

1. Most advisors confuse what's important versus what's urgent on their to-do list. If something is urgent and important, you have to make time for that item. But the items that are not urgent but important set the strategic direction for your practice.

2. Urgent activities help you maintain value; these activities keep all aspects of your practice functioning and moving forward.

3. Important activities are those that create value; these strategic imperatives and objectives are compelling and take your practice to greater heights.

4. You should understand how you use time. Do you prefer a longer, less focused workday, or are you someone who works best in short bursts of activity?

5. Newly minted advisors should focus their efforts more on prospecting than client service. As you become more seasoned, more business will come from existing client referrals, and you'll benefit from spending time with them.

6. You should leverage the 11 x 11 Rule—eleven calls by 11:00 a.m.— to maximize your prospecting efforts. These can be prospects or clients. The key is to place calls that are closest to the money first.

7. You should adopt the 3 x 3 Rule where you set three appointments each day and put three thought pieces into the mail to specific prospects.

8. You should arrange a power hour each day for your prospecting efforts. You should let everyone around you know that this is focused time for you.

9. You should determine where your ideal prospects will be when you decide to call. Make sure your power hour fits with the prospect's schedule.

10. You should evaluate where you are spending your time at least twice per year. As you grow, your method of revenue generation will change based on referrals and reputation.

CHAPTER 5

TAMING SYSTEM STEP 2: WHO'S RIGHT FOR YOU?

I have a good friend that says all the time that there are no such things as coincidences, that is, there's a reason that things happen to us. In the case of writing this chapter, I think that's true. I had lunch recently with a client who has really taken to the advisor job. After sixteen months in the job, she lives the "meaning more" mind-set, really understands the markets, and does a great job of matching solutions to client problems. So during our lunch, we started talking about the clients she was attracting and if an ideal client profile were emerging. She really struggled with the question. After making a few passes through her Rolodex and garnering some really powerful client referrals, there wasn't much of a strategy for the clients she wanted to work with.

At this stage, many advisors find themselves in the same position. Given that this book is really about finding leverage for your growth efforts, here's an early chapter hint. Get really clear on who is ideal for you.

Get really clear on who is ideal for you.

Get clear on how it feels, what it sounds like, what it looks like, and what you are doing when productive with that prospect. Why is this important? It's really a combination of three factors:

1. You have limited time for prospecting. So you don't have time for a trial-and-error approach of any money is good money.

2. As you grow, your best business will come from referrals.

3. Savvy clients will want to know that you have experience in working with clients like them.

So based on that, grab a piece a paper, and start making a list of client types that make sense. Now create another list. Which clients make you cringe when you see them on caller ID? Are they closer to the bottom 10 percent of your book versus the top 10 percent? What do they say? Why do they call? What could you do with the extra time and peace of mind that it takes to service these clients? Make that list now. Here's a sample:

My Ideal Clients	Less-Than-Ideal Clients . . .
understand my process	are confused by my process
respect my time	expect me to drop everything
are inquisitive because they want to learn	are threatened by what they don't know
participate fully in updates	blow off updates routinely
own assets that can be leveraged	have assets that barely approach six figures
give me energy	drain my energy

So what do your two lists look like? Circle some of the commonalities. We'll use these in just a bit. When talking about ideal clients, I typically hear, "I know who my ideal client is. I just need more of them . . . Anyone with $500,000 to invest . . . Successful people entering retirement." At first blush, it all sounds good. These are pretty good profiles, but to land that prospect, you will have to connect with him or her more deeply and uniquely on many more levels. This also assumes you really know who he or she is.

So let's look at some criteria that my clients have said make up a productive client profile:

Fig. 12 Ideal Client Criteria

✕	prior success with this client type and has knowledge of his or her life's work
✕	greater than $2 million in assets to convert
✕	growth opportunity in a managed assets platform
✕	willingness to participate in my firm's diagnostic tool
✕	propensity to partner
✕	needs aligned with solutions I can offer
✕	values contact with key subject-matter experts
✕	receptive to education and professional growth
✕	solution-focused versus product-focused
✕	aligned with how I wish to do business
✕	respectful of me as a person
✕	mindful of my time and my ability to do my best work
✕	curious without being penetrating or challenging
✕	aggressive in recommending me to others

Can you think of any other criteria? If so, think about replacing some of the items on this list so you can keep your focus on a core ten. If you can hit on all ten with a prospect, you're golden!

So now that you have a good list of what would make up an ideal client, let me add another wrinkle. I previously discussed the uniqueness of the buying process in your industry. Anyone worth pursuing is probably working with another advisor. So your entire pursuit will be about change. "So where's the wrinkle?" you might be asking.

What I've learned about human behavior is that humans (with the affluent lumped into that classification) have varying levels of tolerance for change. Some see it as necessary and exciting; others avoid it like the plague, sometimes to their detriment.

**Anyone worth pursuing is working with another advisor.
So your entire pursuit will be about change.**

So in qualifying your ideal prospect you must look at a prospect's capacity and propensity to change. To help advisors through this, we've created a change profiling system that speaks to change adoption. To help advisors manage this dynamic, I've identified five change types:

Fig. 13 Qualifying Your Ideal Prospect: Change Types

The Tiger

New and innovative developments in investing excite this prospect. He sees change as opportunity rather than risk. He is open to meeting with you and learning about your approach. He asks inquisitive and challenging questions based on his own research. He is ready to move quickly and has little interest in kickoffs or group events.

Ways to Work with the Tiger

- Build on his desire for change by being excited during your communications.

- Send him reports and research before your first meeting and frequent updates thereafter.

- Don't tell him how your recommendation can help him. Ask him because he has done his own research and likes to show it off.

Questions to Qualify the Tiger

- What information do you like to have access to when making important financial decisions?

- How did you become so proficient in your knowledge of the markets and investing?

- Where would you want your advisor to fit into your investment decision-making process?

Advantages and Implications for Advisors

These are great clients to work with. As long as you keep them informed, keep your commitments, and maintain a good information flow, they are low maintenance and will remain relatively loyal. They might actually teach you a thing or two in this relationship, and that's a good thing. There's no need to be a smarty-pants here. It actually may backfire on you.

The Eager Beaver

New and beneficial solutions excite this prospect, and she will eagerly be a proponent of your services to her contacts. She is often among the first to adopt new ideas and is eager to share her knowledge and insights with others. She is an excellent role model and communicator. She is excited about being one of the first to do something new and exciting.

Ways to Work with the Eager Beaver

- Emphasize she will be a thought leader among her peers.

- Provide her with information and training to broaden her knowledge, as she will take advantage of all you offer.

- Ask her for her endorsement and referrals to other prospects.

- Have her stand up at your educational events to tell her story.

Questions to Qualify the Eager Beaver

- What gets you most excited about having a plan for your financial future?

- Can you share with me something new that you've added to your method of investing over the past year or two?

- What information, training, or resources would you like to be involved in over the life of your relationship with me?

Advantages and Implications for Advisors

Eager Beavers are the best prospects for obvious reasons. You want to make sure to fully educate this change type on your process so, when shouting from their mountaintop, they're saying the right things and not letting their unbridled enthusiasm dilute any of your credibility or theirs. They will always be looking for the new "new thing," so keep the idea flow rich.

The Wise Owl

This prospect is willing to change with good reason. He is cautious about change unless it is well documented to be workable and worthwhile. Before fully supporting a change, he needs time to think and deliberate. He may eventually come around in order to be accepted by his peers, but at the outset, he sees more risk than opportunity in change. He loves data and research, so ensure this is part of any contact process.

Ways to Work with the Wise Owl

- Stress the benefits of your process and the foundation of your recommendations.

- Keep communication clear and straightforward; synthesize any data or analysis you provide.

- Stay in constant but not oppressive communication, perhaps once per quarter.

- Share success stories frequently.

- Encourage his involvement with Eager Beavers; have him attend joint events or calls.

- Don't push too quickly but inform him when you feel you have left no stone unturned in meeting his requirements.

Questions to Qualify the Wise Owl

- What type of research do you like to do before making big decisions, ones with a significant financial implication?

- Who do you like to consult with when making such decisions? Do you have a thinking partner or two that you trust?

- What information, training, or resources would you like a firm to provide you over the life of their relationship with you?

Advantages and Implications for Advisors

This change type is highly analytical, which provides a great opportunity to inform and educate. It may feel like the prospect is filibustering at times in his requests for data, but don't be alarmed. There is comfort in the details for this change type. But don't let the sales process get too protracted. Be confident to ask for a commitment when you feel you've earned the right.

The Chicken

The name says it all. This prospect is more fearful and skeptical of change and will not change until your recommendation is broadly accepted as proven and the majority of her peers have made a change. She may filter out and distort information you give her. The more you try to convince her, the more she will resist.

A Chicken will typically come around when her important peers start to know about and suggest the change you're recommending.

Ways to Work with the Chicken

- Provide consistent, repeated information about your account transfer process.

- Give regular updates on progress.

- Provide solid business and personal reasons to make a change, appealing to the total person.

- Provide opportunities to connect her with Eager Beavers.

Questions to Qualify the Chicken

- When thinking about investing, whose opinion do you trust the most before making a decision?

- Can you think of a significant change that you've made in your life recently? How did you go about it?

- What value would you place on speaking with some of my existing clients who were in a similar situation to yours?

Advantages and Implications for Advisors

If you have good research at your fingertips combined with solid testimonials, the Chicken can be a valuable prospect.

The Alligator

This prospect's theory is "If it isn't broken, don't fix it." He is also enamored with "the good ol' days." This person has built a successful business or career and sees no reason to change out of his comfort zone with his assets. He doesn't want to tackle anything new that might cause him to have to change his approach. The Alligator will adopt only when it becomes the standard and when changing undeniably outweighs staying the course.

Ways to Work with the Alligator

- Be aware that he will look for ways to stop change and possibly distort the facts.

- Don't ignore his resistance, but consistently and repeatedly state the consequences of not changing.

- Don't spend a lot of time and energy trying to convince Alligators of the merits of changing.

Questions to Qualify the Alligator

- What metrics or gut feeling do you use to determine if your investments are performing as you expect?

- Picking an advisor to work with is a big decision. How did you go about that process with the person you're currently working with?

- What consequences would you like to avoid given your age and goals for retirement?

Advantages and Implications for Advisors

You may be tempted to work with the Alligator, especially if he has sizable assets or engages in serious debate that feels like interest. Be aware that change means loss to the Alligator, and you may wind up spinning your wheels with a prospect that will never commit.

To help you further assess each change type, ask prospects about a really big decision they've made recently and the process they used to get there. This should prove very telling.

Ideal Prospects

A few years back, I created an exercise to help advisors further qualify a quality lead. I called it the Ideal Prospect Qualification Tool. It's designed to help advisors evaluate and qualify ideal prospects based on criteria that are right for them and the prospects they want to attract.

On the worksheet that follows, complete the worksheet using these instructions. (You can also find this on our website at www.4headeddragon. com.)

1. List the prospect or client name. From the list of change types, list his or her type (Tiger, Eager Beaver, Owl, Chicken, or Alligator).

2. Insert the dollar value of the prospect's invested assets and the percent likely to transfer.

3. Note if he or she is using a managed money process and if his or her current advisor relationship is commission or fee-based.

4. On the Ideal Prospect Rating Grid, circle the number that corresponds to your knowledge of the prospect and how he or she compares to your ideal client profile. Place a check mark (√) in the Don't Know box if applicable.

5. For each qualification factor, score that prospect on a scale of one to five with five meaning the prospect exactly meets the criterion and one meaning that he or she does not meet the criterion. Total each row to the right. Note: Feel free to add a profile rating factor or replace an existing factor on our tool. Keep your rating factors to ten.

6. Based on your total score, evaluate the quality of your prospect.

Scoring: The ideal client would have a score of fifty or more.

Fig. 14 The Ideal Prospect Criteria Tool

Rating Your Ideal Prospect

Prospect Name: _____ Client Type: _____

Potential assets to be managed ($): _____ % assets likely to transfer: _____

Is he or she currently using a managed money process? Yes ☐ No ☐

Is current advisor fee-based? Yes ☐ No ☐

Compare to Ideal Client Profile

Circle the number that best corresponds to your knowledge of the prospect and how he or she compares to your ideal client profile. Place a check mark (√) in the "I don't know" cell, if appropriate.

Ideal Prospect Criteria	I don't know / not applicable	Does not meet criteria		Meets criteria somewhat		Exactly meets criteria	Total
Prior success with this client type		1	2	3	4	5	
More than $2 million in assets to convert		1	2	3	4	5	
Growth opportunity in managed asset platform		1	2	3	4	5	
Willing to participate in firm's diagnostic tool		1	2	3	4	5	
Propensity to partner		1	2	3	4	5	
Prospect needs aligned with solutions I can offer		1	2	3	4	5	
Prospect values contact with key SMEs		1	2	3	4	5	
Receptive to education and professional growth		1	2	3	4	5	
Solution-focused versus product-focused		1	2	3	4	5	
Aligned with how I wish to do business		1	2	3	4	5	
Other: _____							
Total Score							

Scoring	
50+	An ideal client
40–49	A high-quality lead
30–39	This will be a longer sale, but you should start making inroads
20–29	Return to this prospect next year and reevaluate
19 or less	Do not pursue

Tool for Assessing Ideal Prospects

So now that you have a profile of your ideal client, you have to put it into words for your network. Your best business will most always come via referral, so you need to help your sources to be clear on who is right for you. A colleague of mine created the following piece for his practice to pass along to his centers of influence and sponsors. I call this the Ideal Client Declaration.

Ideal Client Declaration: Sample

My ideal client is a couple or individual where their primary focus is on their children; funding college and income security are primary concerns. They are younger than age fifty and are in good health. Invested assets are at least $250,000 but ideally $500,000 up to $1 million or more. Regardless of the amount, they are concerned if they will have enough put away by the time they retire after paying for college.

While they are most probably working with an FA, they see the value in seeking an expert in college funding and are open to collaborating. They value a sound process that makes sense, and while accustomed to taking time to think and deliberate, they understand the timing implications of making a decision.

So let's break down this profile into its component parts so you can create one for yourself.

Fig. 15 Creating Your Ideal Client Declaration: Sample

Client Entity	Couple or individual
Focus	Funding college tuition and income security
Age	Younger than age fifty
Health	Good
Invested Assets	At least $500,000 but no less than $250,000
Technical Requirements	Fee-based advisor with access to expertise (for example, funding college tuition)
Relationship Preference	Collaborative
Process Orientation	Pragmatic, deliberate

So let's create your own ideal client declaration. Use the following worksheet to help.

Fig. 16 Ideal Client Declaration Tool

Part 1:

Client Entity	(individual, couple, business)
Focus	(wealth creation, retirement, etc.)
Age	(quote a range)
Health	(condition, time implication if any)
Invested Assets	(suggest a tight range and rationale)
Technical Requirements	(specific expertise)
Relationship Preference	(collaborative or transactional)
Process Orientation	(preferred decision-making process)

Write your ideal client profile declaration here:

So how did you make out? By now, you should be getting a clearer picture of who is ideal for your practice, what it should feel like, and how you can uniquely help this prospect.

Summary

1. Get clear on your ideal prospect: how it feels, what it sounds and looks like, and what you are doing when you're the most productive with these prospects. High-performing advisors are really clear on who is ideal for them.

2. Set criteria for your ideal prospect based on the best clients you're working with and/or how you want it to feel. Criteria can include prior success with this client type, growth opportunity in fees for other services, receptivity to education and professional growth, and respect for you as a person.

3. A high-value prospect is working with someone else. To come to work with you, a prospect needs to feel comfortable with change.

4. There are five change types, and they range in their appetite for change. From strong to weak, the five types are the Tiger, the Eager Beaver, the Owl, the Chicken, and the Alligator.

5. Each change type makes decisions in a different way. To assess a change type, ask about the big decisions he or she has made and the resources he or she has employed in making them.

6. For those with limited time for prospecting, avoid the Chicken and Alligator change types. They will appear to be interested, but change means risk for them.

7. Create an ideal client declaration. You need this for your own efforts as well as those that will recommend you. Literally write out five to six sentences on who is right for you and why.

CHAPTER 6

TAMING SYSTEM STEP 3: TELLING YOUR STORY

I'm a big fan of asking questions. Most people who know me think I'm a genuinely curious person. I find that asking questions stimulates a different part of people's personality and can get people to drop their guard a bit. One of the things I've always been curious about is what clients respond to when selecting an advisor. Is it their overall executive presence, their assets under management, or the firm they work with? Most clients would say it's a smattering of all three. But sophisticated wealthy investors say that it comes down to the advisor's story. Or said another way, their messaging.

In my experience, prospects respond to how an advisor describes situations that prospects can personally relate to and, by doing so, engenders confidence that he or she could credibly and effectively manage their accounts. So this chapter is dedicated to not just creating a pitch but creating messaging that resonates and is aligned with a particular client type.

Messaging is a key component of the Taming process. It's a key component for several reasons:

- Good messaging leads to good prospecting (and more of it).

- Your best clients (your Eager Beavers) need this for their referral activity.

- It's a credibility booster and differentiator, not for what you know but for why others choose you.

- Your message suggests that you've done your homework into that prospect, especially his or her client type.

When speaking of messaging, I recommend clients look at it on three levels: tagline, elevator pitch, and value proposition.

A Tagline

A tagline is a five- to twelve-word descriptor of what you do. In Hollywood, a movie script is typically pitched in twelve words or less. (Look at the movie description next time you download a movie on cable.) For you, it should represent your job function and a particular focus. Here are a few examples. Note the combination of specificity and brevity:

Good: Retirement solution providers for doctors

Better: Retirement solutions for physician groups and their valued employees

Good: Wealth management experts for lawyers

Better: Wealth management solutions for the legal profession

Good: Family solutions for wealth preservation

Better: Helping manage, preserve, and enhance multigenerational wealth

Good: Providing broker/dealer platforms for financial advisors

Better: Helping entrepreneurial financial advisors establish successful businesses

Good: Transfer solutions for business owners

Better: Providing exit strategies and plans for entrepreneurs and their companies

Most of my clients (and businesses, for that matter) try to be too creative in their taglines. The key is to balance describing what you do with the need to communicate what's different. Often, you only need to describe what you do for a particular segment, executives retiring and leaving their employer, for example.

The key is to be specific but not so much so that you close off options for prospects to work with you.

An Elevator Pitch

Once described as the words you'd use if it were just you and your ideal prospect on an elevator to the top floor, this messaging element does a little more than a tagline. At ProDirect, we've adopted an elevator pitch construct from John Orvos, the author of *The Four Faces of Sales*. We call it the I/Why/You pitch.

I/Why/You pitches have three components.

- **I:** who I am and the firm I represent

- **Why:** detail on what I do and why other clients choose to work with me

- **You:** why you, the prospect, might be interested (based on your research)

Here are a few examples of I/Why/You pitches:

Fig. 17 I/Why/You: Sample

Good

I: I'm Ron Hunt from Straightway Financial.

Why: We work with small businesses to help them grow.

You: I thought you'd be interested because growth is the key to your company's future.

Better

I: I'm Ron Hunt, a senior financial planner from Straightway Financial, a planning firm dedicated to the needs of entrepreneurs.

Why: We help leaders of small businesses provide for their future as well as the retirement needs of their employees. Clients work with us for the affordable and easy-to-implement 401(k) plans we provide.

You: I thought you might be interested because the employees of small businesses are often their most important asset. Our solutions help small business leaders reflect that appreciation in the benefits they provide to their employees.

Good

I: I'm Jenny Sturgess with Seacreast Bank.

Why: We provide a full suite of banking services for local businesses.

You: I thought you might be interested because local businesses often have banking needs they are unaware of.

Better

I: I'm Jenny Sturgess from Seacrest Bank, a leader in supporting local businesses in Fairfield County.

Why: We offer custom combinations of banking services to help local businesses not only manage their cash but also deploy their investible assets in the most prudent manner. Clients choose to work with Seacrest for the wide array of services thought only to be available from larger banks.

You: I thought you might be interested because efficiencies in cash management are critical to saving employees' time and improving transaction accuracy. We have specific tools to do just that.

Good

I: I'm Stu Porter from Southern Trust.

Why: We help wealthy individuals with their retirement and wealth transfer needs.

You: I thought you might be interested because the data shows that most people have not saved enough for retirement. We can help show you how much you may need.

Better

I: I'm Stu Porter from Southern Trust, specialists in retirement and multigenerational wealth transfer solutions.

Why: We help the heads of affluent families provide for retirement and craft multigenerational wealth strategies. Clients work with us for the diligence we apply in making sure every family member is taken care of.

You: I thought you might be interested because family dynamics and retirement horizons often present challenging decisions about managing specific assets within an estate. Southern Trust has a specific process for doing this, and I'd welcome the chance to share it with you.

Try your own I/Why/You pitch.

I: _____

Why: _____

You: _____

You can use these I/Why/You pitches when prospecting, opening meetings, and/or educating your centers of influence. Be sure to clearly communicate the benefits that your potential client gets by working with you. This is your credibility kicker. By following the I/Why/You format, you should find it easier to boil down all the complexity of your offer into something that clients and prospects can easily grasp and remember.

Value Proposition

A value proposition is something different. I call this the "two-minute drill." It's a statement that provides the answer to the question, "Can you tell me about you and your firm?" It needs to be very specific. Simply describing the features or capabilities of your offer is not enough. Your value proposition must focus tightly on what your client type wants and values, what problems he or she wants to solve, where he or she wants to improve, or what he or she wants to achieve that's better and faster.

Creating a value proposition has wider application for your practice marketing. Whatever you are selling and to whom, a value proposition is a useful, if not an essential tool. By crafting a value proposition, you're grabbing prospects' attention in such a way that they know "Yes, that's right for me." It also gives your referral base a great story to tell, hopefully often.

Here is a proven and easy way to write your value proposition. Simply answer four questions:

Fig. 18 Value Proposition Framework

1. How do you help clients and people like them?

2. What problems do you solve, and what needs do you address that help your ideal clients reach their goals?

3. What type of impact do you help people and businesses achieve?

4. What can you state that says you understand how to solve the client's problem and you have a special process to do it that your competition doesn't?

Value Proposition Example

1. State how you help clients and people like them:

   At SeaBridge Financial, we help entrepreneurial small business leaders realize their growth plans. Entrepreneurs start their businesses with a different vision of the future than the rest of us. We help them get there.

2. State the problems you solve and the needs you address that help your ideal clients reach their goals:

    Often, these leaders are too busy to focus on their own financial plans and think that every dollar of their capital needs to be put back into the business. What often suffers is a lack of retirement planning and insurance coverage for themselves and their family. Business owners deserve to enjoy the fruits of their labor.

3. State the kind of impact you help people and businesses achieve:

    SeaBridge believes entrepreneurs need to pay themselves first. With resources to create retirement plans and overall financial planning support, we give business owners confidence that they have a sound plan and coverage for all their capital, financial and human.

4. State that you understand how to solve the client's problem and you have a special process to do it that your competition doesn't:

    Our certified financial planners are a rare breed. We're businesspeople first and financial planners second. We leverage our suite of planning tools and market analysis resources to create the right plan for you, your business, and your family.

When to Use Your Messaging

So when should you use this messaging? The quick answer: all the time. Your website, business cards, brochures, postcards, and conversations need to reinforce your messaging. Ensure your tagline is part of your logo. End all articles and blog posts with your value proposition. And equip your centers of influence with your elevator pitch so they can become your de facto sales force. Centers of influence are those people (or organizations) that can boost your market access and credibility through referrals, testimonials, and simple word of mouth. These generally very well-established people are good networkers and can introduce you to the kind of markets (or members) you need and are looking for. Ideally, you should be in the network of several centers of influence. The biggest brands on Wall Street and Main Street spend hundreds of millions of dollars on their messaging. But they don't have the *Dragon* book. Advantage . . . you!

Additional Guidance for When and Where to Use Your Messaging

- **Elevator Pitch:** Use when making your first call, opening meetings, and asking for referrals.

- **The Two-Minute Drill:** Use as your answer to the question, "Can you tell me about what you do?" It's a deeper dive that shifts to your unique capability but speaks to the impact you have (without speaking to financial performance, of course).

- **Tagline:** Preferably use after giving an elevator pitch or two-minute drill. I use it to simplify the message and get to some common ground. But depending on your tagline and how comfortable you are with it, you can use it first.

Summary

1. Messaging is the most important prospecting effort you can engage in. When you have a great message, you want to tell everybody.

2. The converse is true. Without crisp messaging, your prospecting efforts will fail miserably. Get clear on who is right and what they care about, and align your message with that.

3. Effective elevator pitches have 3 parts:

   a. Part one describes who you are and where you are from.

   b. Part two describes what you do and why others made a conscious decision to work with you.

    c.   Part three speaks to your understanding of the prospect's unique situation and that you have insights that your prospect needs to hear about.

4.   There are three types of messaging in the prospecting context: taglines, elevator pitches, and value propositions. None should ever be delivered as a clever quip or gimmick.

5.   A tagline is a ten- to twelve-word description of your offering. Similar to a description of a movie script, it conveys immediate interest and understanding to prospects.

6.   An elevator pitch is used to secure meetings and open sales calls. It's more than a tagline in that it describes the value others derive from working with you.

7.   A value proposition is a four-part framework that provides the answer to the question, "Can you tell me a little about you and your firm?" It communicates what you do, the problems you solve and needs you address, your process for doing it, and the impact it has.

8.   You should use your messaging all the time. Your website, business cards, brochures, postcards, and conversations need to reinforce your messaging. You should ensure your tagline is part of your logo and end all articles and blog posts with your value proposition.

9.   You should equip your centers of influence with your messaging so they can become your de facto sales force.

CHAPTER 7

MAKING CONTACT: MARKETING YOUR PRACTICE

So now you're loaded with a valid set of goals, a laser beam focus on who's ideal for you, and some meaningful messaging. Now it's time to make contact with your market. This chapter will attempt to help you get the message out by excelling at your networking and using some helpful tools to do so. With the advent of social media and digital networking, advisors have never had so many choices for their thought leadership. As mentioned previously, most advisors have limited time for business development. But with a turnkey approach and confidence in the right effort and tools, you can have an impact. So how would you like to get your arms around your market? At a high level, there are four ways to make contact with prospects.

Fig. 19 Contact Approaches

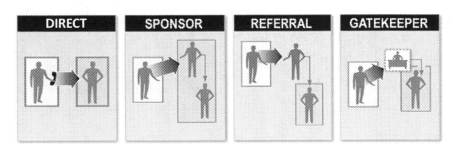

Four Ways to Achieve Prospect Access

- **Direct:** You can go direct to a prospect by calling, e-mailing, writing, or faxing. Typically more grass roots in nature, this method requires that you have dedicated time for prospecting and your messaging is crisp. I have two hints:

- ○ Don't forget the fax. Most faxes get immediately delivered to their intended recipient.

- ○ The office phone is now perceived as a distraction.

- **Sponsor:** This is the best and most reliable form of contact. Sponsorship is similar to a referral but differs in that it typically comes from a credible contact within the prospect's own company, close family, or immediate network. In fact, nearly 70 percent of prospects say they would take a meeting with a salesperson from someone they trust in their own organization or close network.[2] While the most successful approach, sponsorship requires that sponsors be intimate with what you can deliver as well as understand the potential alignment between you and their contact. Sponsorship can come in the form of an e-mail, phone call, or social media mention.

- **Referrals:** Similar to a sponsor, this type of introduction comes from someone outside of the prospect's immediate inner circle or organization. Referrals can be just as powerful, but for referrals to work, your sources should have intimate knowledge of your process and the success you've had with other clients. The other requirement with a referral source is that he or she needs your messaging and the ability to tell it as well if not better than you. Often, the referrer does a good job here because he or she sees your work from afar and can create a more common understanding of what you do. Don't forget family and friends. The folks they send you will most probably lead to a first meeting.

- **Gatekeeper:** Once thought impossible to get around, a gatekeeper can be one of your best sources of support. A gatekeeper can be an administrative assistant, business partner, or even a family member. Bottom line, treat the gatekeeper like the prospect. Err on the side of deference and respect, and give him or her a grounded purpose for your contact. I recommend a format for this I call the RVT, the **r**ationale for the meeting,

---

[2] Dr. Stephen J. Bistritz, *Selling to the C-Suite*, 2009.

the value to the prospect, and the test for understanding and agreement. You also want to let the gatekeeper know how you came to the prospect. Use his or her name as often as you can in the dialogue without sounding repetitive. The key in working with the gatekeeper is to trade on your respect and purpose to ask for something tangible. That could be a meeting or the best time to call back. Always get the gatekeeper's full contact info and let him or her know how the meeting went when you indeed land it. Follow up with a handwritten note. Why? Your competition is not doing this and everyone loves a handwritten note.

- **Social Media:** Howard Howell, Internet sales consultant, said, "Use social media to engage people. Grow your network. Give generously and people will follow you." Social media takes on many different forms, including Internet forums, weblogs, social blogs, microblogging, wikis, podcasts, photographs or pictures, video, rating, and social bookmarking. In other words, social media is media designed for social interaction using highly accessible and scalable communication techniques. Social media is the use of web-based and mobile technologies to turn communication into interactive dialogue.

Nearly half of US FAs now use social media daily to interact with clients, according to Accenture's report, "Closing the Gap: How Tech-Savvy Advisors Can Regain Investor Trust (2013)." The same study noted that 40 percent of FAs had gotten new clients through Facebook, 25 percent through LinkedIn, and 21 percent through Twitter.

The important thing to know is that it's not just millennials using social media to gather information. Skill and comfort levels are increasing among clients in their sixties and seventies because social media is the way they communicate with their families around the world.

You need a social media presence. The average adult looks at his or her smartphone 150 times per day (Pew Research 2013). Plus, online brokers are gathering assets faster than full service firms. But to have a presence in social media, you first need to check your firm's social media policy.

Many firms do not permit advisors to use Facebook. As for LinkedIn, they provide strict guidelines as to what information you can provide and how you connect with others. While company compliance policies do not appear to deter overall social media adoption among advisors, the policies do affect how advisors can leverage social networks for business.

These restrictions typically prohibit advisors from performing certain actions on LinkedIn such as requesting or writing recommendations, posting to groups or pages, or sending InMail within LinkedIn. If your firm does allow you a LinkedIn presence, by all means establish a profile there. To protect yourself, add a disclaimer to your social media profiles that tells everyone that nothing you say should be construed as investment advice.

To be found as an FA, you need to know how the world of social media and web search works. Google is the leading search engine, and it features bots that scour the Internet for new information. These Google bots troll the pages of LinkedIn, Facebook, and Twitter looking for new content. If the bot finds new content, the bot comes back more often. As with keywords, search engines like sites with fresh content. While blogging is a great way to get picked up by search engines, regulations for advisors' sites around dynamic (blogs) content versus static (web and Facebook pages) differ. So in all cases, defer to your firm's social media compliance policy.

LinkedIn

FAs know that winning and retaining clients relies heavily on networks and referrals. LinkedIn can help in that regard. Nearly three out of four FAs use at least one social network for business. And among these, nine in ten use LinkedIn. Even more importantly, more than 60 percent of those who prospected on LinkedIn successfully gained new clients as a result, with nearly a third of these generating a million dollars or more in assets under management (LinkedIn, "FTI Study," 2012). LinkedIn helps advisors establish a professional profile online, stay in touch with clients, and find experts, ideas, and opportunities. As a selling tool, it can make the cold call immediately warm.

The first step to getting started with LinkedIn is to set up a profile:

1. Go to www.linkedin.com, and click Join now.

2. Compile your profile. Write a description that tells people who you are, where you're from, and what you do. Ensure it provides an accurate reflection of your skills, expertise, and role. Include a professional quality photograph of yourself and concise information in the Summary section. Be credible, and list as many qualifications and certifications as possible in keeping with your firm's compliance policy. Get as much detail into your Experience section as possible, but no puffery. For advisors, be sure not to speak to performance or allude to future performance. Include a link to your Facebook business page.

3. Network. The more connections you have, the more likely you are to be found by people who can help you. But remember that networking is a giving game, so make sure your overall presence on LinkedIn emphasizes what you have to share more than what you need from others. Keep your connections as relevant as possible, and be mindful of accepting contact requests unless you can see a mutual benefit. I tend not to accept requests from those who are trolling the site and don't have time to even make the briefest inquiry or comment in their request. Search for people you know by name and/or company, and make quick connections with existing colleagues and current business contacts. Use the e-mail account tools to search for LinkedIn users within your personal e-mail lists. When making a connection, select the option that best resembles how you know this person and then send a short, personal message inviting him or her to connect. Be honest. If you're not, LinkedIn will begin asking for the e-mail of the contact you're trying to reach. To increase the reach of your own personal network, browse your contacts' connections. I like seeing who others allow into their network. LinkedIn will calculate a degree of connection (first, second, and third tier) so you can start with common connections for making new contacts. When asking your first-degree contacts to introduce you to a second-degree contact, provide the reason and the value to the targeted contact for doing so.

4. Join LinkedIn groups. LinkedIn allows you to join groups in the areas in which you operate. Being in a group allows you to search for people you want to contact and get in touch for free via LinkedIn messages. Because you belong to the same group,

you are likely to get a reply. The key to joining a group is to be a net "giver." That is, make sure you are contributing more than you are taking. You can do this by posting links to news articles and starting new discussions. This gets to the heart of my philosophy about LinkedIn as a lead generation tool. I advise clients to use LinkedIn as a venue for trading influence and insight versus touting their own capability or always going to the well for help.

Facebook

If your firm allows a Facebook presence, establish a Facebook business page. A Facebook business page is an important digital reputation tool for your practice. The link to your page will rank in search engines, and the page can showcase your practice. A Facebook presence is important for a consistent presence across all of your digital assets: your website, LinkedIn profile, and Facebook business page. Even if you never populate your page with updates, it is still an important search engine asset. To build your own page, go to https://www.facebook.com/business/build and follow the instructions.

Once you set up your business page, you will need to build a community of fans. It will be important to update your page frequently and consistently to foster engagement with your desired audience. The goal is to get fans to link to your site, not to garner testimonials from them. To build fans for your page, here are a few ideas for you:

- Send an e-mail to your list of clients, prospects, and professional contacts, asking them to join your community on Facebook. (Be sure to tell them the benefits of doing so.)

- Send an update to your connections on your personal Facebook profile announcing your page and what they will find there.

- If your firm allows it, place a Facebook fan box on your blog or website.

- Share your Facebook page posts across your other social networks, such as LinkedIn.

- Share the whole you. Don't just share financial insights on your business page. Share information about community involvement, speaking engagements, and/or community events.

- Use photos and videos to tell your story.

Keep in mind that a Facebook business page is not a substitute for your website and cannot offer financial advice or recommendations.

Twitter

Twitter completes the triumvirate of the top business social media sites. Most companies do not allow Twitter as part of their social media policy, and I personally am not a huge fan of the medium for professional networking. But if you do sign up for an account, I prefer to see advisors use Twitter to direct contacts to their website, LinkedIn, or Facebook business page. Twitter can also be a useful tool for promoting free webinars, white papers, workshops, videos, and educational tips and, in the meantime, expanding your prospect list. I also coach clients to use Twitter to pose questions to foster discussion. But in all cases, do not fall into the immediacy trap of Twitter. Stay away from Twitter in times of stress or when you're tired or emotional. Use it as the business tool that it is. To sign up, simply go to www.twitter.com. And in all cases, consult your firm's social media policy before establishing a Twitter account.

Lead Generation: What's Old Can Be New

With Rolodexes, Microsoft Outlook, and social media, lead sources abound. No matter what the platform, advisors need introductions to grow their practice. From current clients, introductions from other advisors that don't compete in your space, educational workshops, or your own networking efforts in social and traditional media, it's important to get the right word out.

The high-performing advisors I work with are ultra creative in the types of lead-generation methods they use. They have a sense of what their target prospects are responding to and invest accordingly. In the past few years, prospects have opted out of face-to-face events, preferring to do their research online and to see their family for a change. But I see the pendulum swinging in the other direction as prospects and clients want more face-to-face contact for assurance.

According to ClientWise, a financial advisor coaching and research firm, 71 percent of new client introductions originate from just two sources: loyal client advocates and other trusted advisors. So the key with any type of lead generation is to cultivate these two sources while filling in the other 29 percent with other viable sources.

Lead generation is a giving game.

Just as on LinkedIn, you need to be a net giver when cultivating leads. It's just the way the universe works. As one of our top sales coaches says, "A giving hand is always full." Here is a short list of lead sources outside of LinkedIn and Facebook that can help you add more prospects. You've probably thought about many of these already. The key is to use the asset that you created, which is your messaging, to maximize the impact of your efforts in these activities:

1. Rent out a movie theater so prospects can enjoy the latest family-friendly film with their kids.

2. Become a certified sommelier.

3. Join the local club chapter of Porsche, BMW, or any other fine automobile.

4. Own something of value and join the related affinity organizations associated with it. For example, antique cars, guns, and antique jewelry are good places to start.

5. Attend the business development road shows of large accounting firms.

6. Speak before the most visible clubs and organizations in a fifty-mile radius.

7. Start a visible community project, and solicit the help of others.

8. Host educational workshops for a small number of clients and their invited guests (fifteen attendees maximum and investment topics not necessary).

9. Attend the charitable fund-raisers of organizations whose board members fit your ideal client profile.

10. Try skeet shooting and be interested in others' guns. A story is attached to every piece.

11. Attend the Show House events of the local Junior League chapter.

12. Attend awards ceremonies for service organizations.

13. Join a luncheon club.

14. Give a talk to an investment club.

15. Attend local land trust solicitation events.

16. Attend a golf or tennis camp. Ask them who their ideal camper is.

17. Participate in a walkathon for a cause you believe in.

18. Use mileage awards to travel first class. Always.

19. Leverage the networks of your attorney, CPA, and insurance agent. Have something to offer them.

20. Teach a course at a local college that values the perspective of adjunct professors.

21. Attend gallery openings and museum parties that support young artists. Connoisseurs like to give a leg up to new talent.

22. Join an arts board that supports mediums you're fond of.

23. Sponsor a sports team in a local affluent area, especially girls' sports.

24. Hang out at the local coffee shop and meeting place of a large corporation or hospital.

25. Host an event at one of your favorite fine dining restaurants. Raffle the opportunity to dine at the chef's table.

26. Get to know one of your local journalists by taking him or her to lunch. Offer him or her ideas.

27. Attend the Heckerling Institute on Estate Planning annual conference.

28. Get to know exit planning specialists. Business owners will often want to reinvest a portion of the proceeds from the sale of their business.

29. Befriend your local Rolex technician (www.awci.com).

30. Host a wine tasting. Invite guests to share their treasured labels.

You only want to have people come to something, chat with you, and get to know you so they feel comfortable. Keep in mind that your competition is doing many of these same things. They're showing up and offering as well as asking for referrals. You have to be better. Be crisper with your messaging and more fluent in prospects' issues, pressures, and aspirations. Get in the habit of helping others first. Remember, a giving hand is always full.

So how do you do this? When meeting people at these events, forget about being interesting. Be interested. People value the interest that others take in their hobby or passion. Meaning more to clients is about getting others to not only talk about their passion but to earn the right to share yours and the reason why you became a financial professional. Then using what you learned by being interested, you deliver your I/Why/You pitch and let the law of reciprocity kick in.

Lead Conversion: More Is Not Always More

So now that you've chosen the contact approach that's right for you and your top prospects, you're ready to reach out. Please know that more will not be more. More calls, more e-mails, more faxes, and more collateral will not get it done. Instead, it has to be a coordinated effort of all those elements guided by three things:

1. Fit with your ideal prospect profile

2. High-level identification of a problem worth solving in the eyes of the prospect

3. Your ultimate meeting objective

These three things should guide any outreach campaign. So why do I recommend multiple touches or interactions with prospects? Our research at ProDirect shows that it takes six to seven touches to convert a lead to a prospect. A touch could be an invitation to an event, a faxed article of interest, or a handwritten note introducing yourself. I believe a lead to be someone with the characteristics of your ideal profile in your target demographic.

A prospect is more than that. This person is someone in your target demographic who has expressed a need and is open to learning more. The good news is that your competition stops at three touches. This means that you need to again be clear on an ideal prospect profile and align your touches around that. The key is to ensure your touches are both varied and valuable in the eyes of the prospect.

Fig. 20 The Seven-Touch Strategy

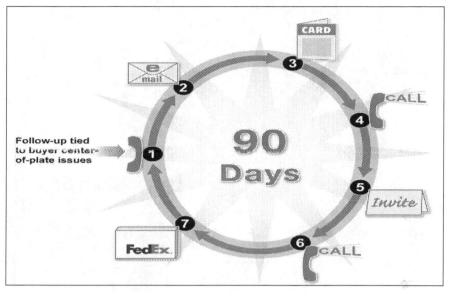

Use Multiple Touches to Achieve Differentiated Access

Think of this process like a mini ad campaign. Like the hottest cell phone, you'll see it on TV, Facebook, Twitter, a billboard, and the back of a city bus. The message reaches you through a stream of consciousness. Your touch strategy will do the same for your prospect. You can use the following sample touches to shape your seven-touch strategy.

Fig. 21 Sample Touch Menu

Phone call	Thank you note
Fax	Book of interest
Email – invitation to a community event or industry forum	CD series for car
	Satisfaction survey
Invite to topical webinar or web conference	Article of interest
Newsletter	Referral for THEIR business
Positive press about your firm	Educational offerings
Charitable contribution	Call report from past meeting

Sample 7-Touch Strategy

The key is to select touches that you can execute and deliver value to the prospect. A quick word about touches: keep in mind that you are going after smart, successful people, those who have made a living being right. When planning for touches that include information or articles, help your prospect avoid being wrong.

If you're sending an analyst report, add a contrarian viewpoint. And when sending information, synthesize it for the prospect and highlight key areas. Savvy prospects do take time to read timely and targeted information, especially Tigers. Let's look at an actual seven-touch plan that one of our clients created. Certain details have been changed or modified to protect the innocent.

Fig. 22 7-Touch Planning Tool: Sample

Seven-Touch Strategy for Lajolla Medical (Dr. Cheri Santi, COO)

My Seven-Touch Goal for Next Ninety Days: See Me as Viable Resource for 401(k) Plan

Touch #: Day in Cycle	Specific Touch	Date	By Whom	Intended Outcome	Results
1 Day 1	FedEx intro letter	1/15	Me	Introduce me/the firm	Prospect admin acknowledged receipt
2 Day 13	Webinar invite (via e-mail)	1/28	Admin	Share trends from midmarket pension conference	Accepted invite via Outlook
3 Day 26	E-mail firm success stories	2/10	Me	Give Dr. Santi confidence in our ability in the health-care space	Outlook read receipt received
4 Day 39	Handwritten note	2/23	Me	To compel Dr. Santi to meet with our team	N/A
5 Day 52	Call (after rounds)	3/8	Me	To connect on all touches to date and ask for a meeting	Prospect agreed to meeting
6 Day 65	Fax agenda	3/21	Admin	Solicit feedback on agenda	Prospect added item regarding investment choice
7 Day 78	E-mail: Premeeting call invite	4/3	Admin	Connect Dr. Santi and others on team to prep for in-person meeting	Had a good call. Dr. Santi connected well with product team
Opportunistic Ad hoc Touch	Meeting Recap	4/16	Me	Solidify key points discussed in meeting	Invited to bid/finals process

So here are the steps to create and execute an effective Seven-Touch Strategy:

1. Create a strategic touch goal. What impression do you want to make on this prospect? What is his or her client type?

2. Choose seven to ten touches from the ProDirect Touch Menu in figure 21. Don't be limited by what I've shared with you. Be creative and align with potential prospect interests.

3. Schedule, space accordingly, and assign touch responsibility (approximately one touch every thirteen days). It can actually work to your advantage to have others participate in the touch process.

4. Project your intended outcome for each touch, and track your results.

Most advisors find it helpful to start with five prospects on a seven-touch strategy with a maximum of twenty once you're comfortable with the rhythm and level of your involvement.

Try creating one for a high-value prospect on your pipeline.

Seven-Touch Strategy for _____

My Seven-Touch Goal Over Next Ninety Days: _____
_____

Touch #: Day in Cycle	Specific Touch	Date	By Whom	Intended Outcome	Results
1 Day 1					
2 Day 13					
3 Day 26					
4 Day 39					
5 Day 52					
6 Day 65					
7 Day 78					
Opportunistic Ad hoc Touch					

Summary

1. Marketing your practice has to be multidimensional. Choose a blend of live events, webinars, and social media.

2. At a high level, there are four ways to make contact with prospects when marketing your practice: direct, sponsorship, referral, and through a gatekeeper.

3. Social media is a powerful tool for advisors with the most popular outlets being LinkedIn and Facebook. Nearly three out of four FAs use at least one social network for business. And among these, nine in ten use LinkedIn.

4. No matter what the medium, you should always abide by your firm's social media policy. You should avoid giving and receiving testimonials, referrals, or direct investment advice of any kind.

5. Networking is a giving game. If you help others, the universe will reward you. Be a thought leader in chat rooms and groups when using social media.

6. If you prefer live events, you should ensure the topic and venue align with a prospect's client type. When meeting people at these events, you should forget about being interesting. Be interested.

7. A lead is someone with the characteristics of your ideal profile in your target demographic. A prospect is more than that. This person is someone in your target demographic who has expressed a need and is open to learning more.

8. For lead generation, more is not always more. More calls, more e-mails, more faxes, and more collateral will not get it done. Instead, it has to be a coordinated effort of all those elements.

9. Our research at ProDirect shows that it takes six to seven touches to convert a lead to a prospect. A touch could be an invitation to an event, a faxed article of interest, or a handwritten note introducing yourself.

10. Most advisors find it helpful to start with five prospects on a seven-touch strategy with a maximum of twenty once you're comfortable with the rhythm and level of your involvement.

CHAPTER 8

TAMING SYSTEM STEP 4: DESIGNING CONVERSATIONS

The high-performing advisors we coach trade on the special needs and knowledge they each bring to prospects as a person and as a financial professional. We'll also look at contact in two ways to keep it simple: opening and closing.

The whole purpose of your activity up to this point was to drive more activity with qualified ideal prospects within a limited time budget. Social media, e-mail, referrals, and events are all important, but none more so than the face-to-face meeting. So much value has to be communicated in a short time, and your prospect is making snap judgments about you. With so much pressure to make the in-person interaction work, we believe that advisors need to actually design the conversation.

Designing the conversation is about controlling the process of how you want the interaction to go. This is more than just opening, advancing, and concluding a meeting. Rather, it's an intentional process of priming a dialogue that solicits prospect input, input you can do something with. At this stage, the prospect's spoken words are gold, and you'll actually use them to shape a recommended next step.

Designing the conversation is about controlling the process of how you want the interaction to go.

Think of discovery meetings in two stages: connecting, rapport building, and light fact-finding in initial meetings; and clarification, options testing, and opinion seeking in subsequent meetings. But in all cases, your meaning more mind-set needs to seep through your agenda and your approach.

Initial Meetings

Designing conversations is about discovery done differently. Savvy prospects don't want to spend all their time educating you on their situation, but as an advisor, it's important to secure a certain amount of information to support future dialogue. In first meetings, it's important to assess a client type right away and shape your questions accordingly.

For example, a newly married professional couple in the process of bringing their lives together (which were both done solo up to this point) has many decisions to make, particularly around wealth management and personal finances. In your precall research, you might check each person's profile on LinkedIn to look at past employers to get a handle on how many jobs (and perhaps 401(k)s he or she has had). You'd also want to conduct a web search for trends in comingling finances. This is a tricky example, and it can be polarizing.

Some people want to preserve what they had coming into a marriage, that is, what they've accumulated before they became a couple or a family. Having separate accounts gives some level of comfort and peace of mind knowing that "what was mine remains mine." However, some believe that having separate accounts discourages the development of shared financial goals. No matter what the issue, you need to know the prospect's hot buttons.

In your initial meeting, you would want to answer these questions:

- How is the comingling process going (not just finances)?

- What has been your most meaningful accomplishment together thus far?

- What goal do you both want to strive for together?

- What remains as your next big decision?

- What decision would give you both the greatest comfort to have behind you?

Prospects in this situation want to feel that they are not alone and they've done at least something good in their attempt to solidify a joint financial future.

One of the biggest challenges I hear our advisor clients say is that getting the second meeting is often harder than securing the first. To set yourself up for second meeting success, follow these guidelines:

- Your first meeting needs to start with an agenda and a purpose.

- If your meeting is scheduled for an hour, you need to protect the last fifteen minutes to summarize what you've learned, reconnect back to the purpose of the meeting, and recommend a productive next step for both parties.

- Typically, three to four action items will arise after every meeting. Listen for those in your dialogue, and focus on them during your recap.

- You should make the value of the second meeting tangible for the prospect.

Next Meetings

Your second meeting and those thereafter should act as a cumulative stream of value. Each meeting should build to a next better meeting that gets you both closer to some form of commitment. One of the best ways to kick off second meetings is to recap the first and let the prospect know you were thinking about him or her and have some additional thoughts. Bring forth another agenda and gain agreement on the meeting's purpose.

What I am recommending will help you avoid stalled opportunities. At each interaction, a prospect needs to feel that he or she is getting value, especially if he or she is with another advisor and contemplating a change. If not, you are just another pitch to the prospect.

At some point during the second meeting, share examples of other clients who were in a similar situation and what was important to them during this time. This earns you the right to make a recommendation later and relates that you have the experience to handle his or her situation. It also gives you the chance to assess the priority of taking action. I coach my clients to look at next meetings as more of a validation and affirmation process than pure discovery. In the prospect's mind, the treadmill is already running, and the expectation is that you will match his or her speed in your interactions.

In other words, the second stage of designing conversations is questions light and clarification heavy. While you can't totally predict meeting outcomes, you can control the process of interactions that help put you in a position to make an intelligent recommendation.

In the prior example, the next meeting should feature the following:

- a recap of the first meeting and a successful completion of the agenda

- additional thoughts that you had post-session

- a list of issues for newly married couples to consider (from a third party)

- two to three focus areas based on the answers to the questions I recommended earlier for meeting one

In all cases, you will state a purpose for the meeting and check in with the prospect to make sure it's the right path. Depending on the time in between meetings and additional thoughts that all parties might develop, there might be a shift in priority or a need to go deeper in a particular area.

The term *intelligent recommendation* comes from the fact that you're combining your prepursuit research and the prospect's spoken words around his or her needs to offer a solution. This isn't about features and benefits or death by questioning. Rather, designing conversations is about aligning your practice solution with the client type issues at hand. Features and benefits act to reinforce how your recommendation works and prove that your recommendation is sound. So let's take a look at a model that can put this all in place for you. I've looked at every conversation model out there, and here is what I came up with.

Fig. 23 The Prospect Conversation

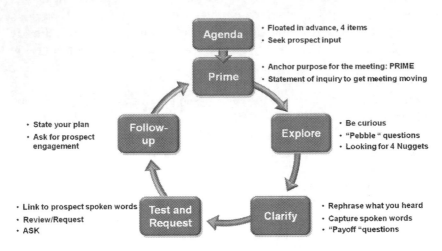

Process for Designing the Conversation

This process is designed to help you connect with, validate, and affirm smart, successful people. Remember that anyone who is someone worth working with has found success and blazed his or her own path to get there. It's not about telling, selling, and death by questioning. Instead, it's a conversation that you design and initiate to get the prospect sharing privileged insights, ones that will shape the tee-up of your solution. Really what you're doing is validating a hypothesis you had about how you could help the prospect based on his or her client type.

So let's break down the prospect conversation:

1. **Agenda:** Preparing an agenda is a lost art. This is where prospect engagement starts. Float an agenda via e-mail in advance and ask the prospect to add or subtract from the list. Take the feedback you get, and put your agenda on your best letterhead. Most of the time, the prospect will write on this in your meeting.

2. **Prime:** Priming the conversation is a bold thesis statement or purpose of the meeting. We also call it the RVT, **r**ationale for the meeting, the **v**alue to the prospect, and a **t**est for relevance. The

last ten years saw too many advisors putting this in the hands of the prospect in the spirit of the relationship.

3. **Explore:** This is typically your first meeting or two, where you're asking questions. It isn't a laundry list of questions. It's two types of questions that get the prospect to add color to his or her problem and a level of intensity around doing something about it. Here are a few examples related to the commingled finances example we've been discussing:

    Pebble Question: What has been the hardest part about bringing your finances together since you got married this summer? (You're looking for issues around paperwork, asset allocation anxiety, or a total lack of attention to the issue.)

    Payoff Question: If we could find a way to easily convert and combine a small percentage of your assets into a jointly owned mutual fund that would provide immediate asset allocation protection, what comfort would that give, relative to the other perfect union issues you're facing right now? (This question gets the prospect to articulate a degree of comfort about taking a good first step toward managing comingled finances.)

4. **Clarify:** The key to prospect conversations is to make sure the other party feels heard and understood. For you, it's about making sure you've got the facts straight and you're clear about the prospect's perception of an issue or problem. It also gives you a window into the prospect's readiness to take action. Remember, these conversations are your time too. By following this process, you earn yourself the right to ask for some form of prospect opinion or, better yet, commitment. When in this step, keep testing until the prospect says, "Yes, that's right." If that doesn't work, go back and ask another pebble question that the prospect can easily identify with and expand upon. This may even lead to a better recommendation in the end.

    Example: "So what I hear you saying is that a pre-asset-allocated mutual fund would be a big help, especially now with the laundry list of shared duties you must have. Sounds like it would be a great relief to have some part of your finances on autopilot right now. Is that right?" (In this case, you are validating the prospect by letting him or her know that you heard him or her and testing that your recommendation is a high priority versus the myriad of other details to be managed with two people entering into marriage.)

Keep in mind that, during any meeting, four to five truly viable points will ring out from the conversation. Too many advisors get caught up in capturing every thought in their notes or, worse yet, fail to capture the real essence of what matters most to the prospect. This happens because most of us don't want to miss anything. But often, it's because advisors want to close as soon as possible, and we're looking for the right cues to make a product recommendation. Advisors should be listening for cues to shape a solution recommendation based on the client type (newly married couple), his or her problems, and where the prospect is saying he or she needs relief from the pebble in his or her shoe. Remember this. When you're writing, you're not connecting.

The following tool can help you capture the most important details in your next meeting. Focus less on taking notes and more on the confidence that four to five items will fall out of your next conversation. You'll be ready.

Fig. 24 Meeting Recap Tool: Sample

Meeting Recap Tool: Capturing the Nuggets
Prospect: Premier Urology Associates, Dr. Keenan **Date:** 2/13/13 **Meeting Purpose:** Discuss Dr. Keenan's role in providing deferred compensation and benefits to his peers.
Nugget 1: Came together due to physicians' needs to protect their income, to distribute the cost of running their practice across many doctors, and to serve patients reliably and well.
Nugget 2: Given greater scale (fifty urologists in the group), provide for the ability to invest in leading-edge technologies.
Nugget 3: Want to fund the group's application of the most innovative and exciting technologies available in the field of urology and utilize a state-of-the-art electronic medical records system.
Nugget 4: Group physicians willing to invest in the practice, but they want the benefit of a sound retirement and profit-sharing plan. It's a board decision, but they are looking at ideas right now.
Summary: While the end game is the pension and profit-sharing plan, insights to build the relationship need to include best practices for the right kind and right pace of infrastructure investments to make without sacrificing care or the group's earnings.

5. **Test and Request:** Here, you want to begin recommending your solutions to prospects. At this stage of the meeting, you're testing a few ideas by playing back what you heard in your initial meeting and offering a range of solutions. This gives the prospect

confidence that you were listening and you're staying in alignment with his or her decision process up to this point. Keep in mind that these ideas are aligned with a client type (for example, newly married couple, retired executive, or express lube franchise owner). Ideas for the prior newly married couple example could include providing a prospectus for asset-allocated mutual funds or information on target date retirement funds that automatically and gradually decrease the stock allocation and increase the bond and cash allocation as the fund approaches a target date, say, 2030.

The request part is a request for the prospect's opinion and feedback. Prospects typically buy in to what they have a hand in creating, so do not skip this step. Most prospect procrastination comes from the fact that they didn't achieve enough clarity and input throughout the sales process. At this stage, you'd rather surface any concerns now than sit around for a month waiting for a prospect to call you back.

Sample Test and Request Language

So what I think I hear you saying is that this is a great time to put a piece of your combined financial future on autopilot right now. At this point, what I'd like to suggest is a combined $50,000 investment in one of our balanced funds. I also suggest a Target Date Fund as well for retirement. We have a great 2030 fund solution. With the target date fund, we can start with just 25 percent of each of your individual portfolios and increase that amount at a pace that feels comfortable for both of you. I'd be glad for your thoughts on this approach.

Hint

Rough layouts sell better than final ones. You are testing ideas, not the final product. If you start talking solution too soon, it may seem too final too early for the prospect. So let him or her be a part of shaping what's next. At this stage, you only need to give him or her a few viable options and ask for an increasingly higher level of commitment. Be his or her thinking partner, not a vendor.

Follow-Up

Hopefully if you've been doing all that we've talked about in the book, this is an easy step for you. But many advisors struggle here. The nature of follow-up then needs to move from just checking in to something more meaningful.

We hear all the time about the great series of meetings an advisor has had with a prospect: strong personal connection, high interest level, and an intense curiosity about your process. Then nothing. Phone calls and e-mails never get returned, and all of a sudden, it feels like you're stalking.

> **The nature of follow-up then needs to move from just checking in to something more meaningful.**

Your ideal prospect has people following up on him or her all day long. The key is to make the next step in the relationship specific when you're in the meeting and to get the next one on the calendar. This isn't a tactical recommendation; it's a nod to all advisors that you control the process. Follow-up should be a valuable add-on to the conversation that either validates the approach you recommended or gives the prospect additional confidence to take action.

Designing Conversations and Change Types

Hopefully by now, it's becoming clearer how to design conversations based on a client type. Newly married couples will have different needs and thus expectations of you than the patriarch of a large family looking to provide for multigenerational wealth. In all cases, you are sending an agenda in advance and priming the meeting with a purpose that's relevant to the client type and his or her appetite for change.

The following grid has some hints on how best to design conversations with the various change types we discussed in chapter 5:

Fig. 25 Change Types Meeting Set-Up

Change Type	First Interaction (Phone v. Face-to-Face)	Priming Question or Statement for Meeting Kickoff	Areas to Probe	Areas to Avoid
Tiger	Whichever is most convenient because Tigers are self-assured	• Question • Tigers are confident and know what they want from meetings	• Research they've conducted • Their hypothesis at this stage	• Jumping in too soon with ideas • Neglecting their knowledge
Eager Beaver	Face-to-face because you play on their excitement for what's next and what's possible	• Statement • They see you as the expert	• Areas that get them the most excited • Their vision	• None (but keep the prospect focused)
Owl	Whichever is most convenient for the Owl because they are analytical and respond well to data	• Question • They are analytical and respond well to inquiry	• Their thought process • Frequently referenced data sources • The way they make decisions	• Infinite loops of data • Proof points
Chicken	Face-to-face because the Chicken needs comfort and reassurance	• Statement • This breeds confidence	• What their most trusted peers are doing • Their last big decision	• Closing statements because they need to be brought along slowly
Alligator	Phone because you must always qualify an Alligator and use your time wisely	• Question • You should always test the Alligator around his or her plan	• Their comfort level with the status quo • The consequences of not changing	• An argument of minor points because they will try to take you off track and question your approach

Contact Etiquette

Be mindful of the following tips when connecting with high-value prospects. These are as much tips as they are expectations that high-value prospects have of service providers:

- Don't go overboard with courtesy or dramatic displays of respect. It won't be valued, and it's just not necessary.

- When you first speak with a prospect on the phone, say, "It's nice to speak with you" rather than "It's nice to meet you." You may have spoken or met with this person in the past, and it saves embarrassment later. Plus, this tactic puts you on equal stature with the prospect.

- When meeting face-to-face, the same rule applies. Your greeting should be "Nice to see you" instead of "Nice to meet you." Again, it puts you on equal stature.

- Always send an agenda in advance and ask for input. This starts engagement early. During the meeting, bring the agenda in hard copy on your very best letterhead. This is usually what your prospect will take notes on. If the client objects, simply use yours as a guide for the meeting.

- Structure your phone calls and meetings with three phases: Opening, Advance, and Close. Your meeting should start with an acknowledgment of how you met, the agreed-upon purpose of the meeting, and some reference to the prospect's client type or situation.

- Recognize that the path of the meeting follows the path of the solution hypothesis you've been proving throughout the sales process.

- Recognize the close is some mutually beneficial next step, options you're prepared to offer that advance the relationship.

- Prime your conversations. That is, get the car started with a statement or question that gets the meeting off to a great start around the purpose and hopeful outcome. Ask for feedback on the meeting's purpose and proceed.

- Once you have a sense of the client type and problem, shift into hurt-and-rescue mode with your pebble and payoff questions. Drill down on what the prospect sees as a pebble in his or her shoe and the value of doing something about it.

Summary

1. Face-to-face interactions need to be treated like gold. The best meetings have prospect engagement written all over them.

2. Designing the conversation is about controlling the process of how you want the interaction to go. This is more than just opening, advancing, and concluding a meeting. Rather, it's an intentional process of priming a dialogue that solicits prospect input, input you can do something with.

3. You should solicit an agenda in advance, prime the meeting opening with a powerful focus, and ask clarifying and needs-seeking questions that stimulate thought on the part of the prospect.

4. The prospect conversation should happen in six steps: Float an agenda in advance; prime the conversation with your objective and the connection to a prospect need; ask pebble questions to get at "what's not quite right" in the prospect's world; clarify what you heard and ask a payoff question, one that gets the prospect to articulate the value of taking action; test an idea and approach and request some feedback on it; and set an expectation for follow-up.

5. Once you have a sense of the client type and problem, you should shift into hurt-and-rescue mode with your pebble and payoff questions. Drill down on what the prospect sees as a pebble in his or her shoe and the value of doing something about it.

6. With the Designing Conversations process, you should check in with the prospect at each step to ensure understanding and engagement. This keeps concerns or reservations from building up and makes your closing process a lot easier at the end.

7. The nature of follow-up then needs to move from just checking in to something more meaningful.

8. During any meeting, four to five truly viable points will ring out from the conversation. Don't get caught up in capturing every thought in your notes or, worse yet, fail to capture the real essence of what matters most to your prospect.

CHAPTER 9

CLOSING AND GAINING COMMITMENT

I'm sure many of you looked at the table of contents and came to this chapter first. As a salesperson, I know I would. We all need more closing activity. But to sustain your success, all elements of the Taming model need to be executed fully to bring the results you desire.

Please note that no clever quip, phrase, or persona will help you close wealthy prospects. Not in your industry. To be successful, you'll need to validate and affirm your prospects, to make them feel that they have been heard and understood. In the last chapter, we talked about the value of designing the conversation you want to have.

These conversations address a particular client type, their associated problems and needs, and their view of their situation. In these conversations, high-performing advisors are asking for their point of view on the potential solutions you recommend. By doing this, you're earning the right to make an intelligent recommendation. Similar to the change types we meet with, we need to be mindful of the client type. The following tips are how to make your closing efforts more productive with different client types. I've provided some clues as to how to conduct meetings later in the sales process and areas to reinforce and avoid with specific client types. In all cases, the areas to reinforce should include the spoken words around what the prospect (client type) said about the value of solving their problem.

Fig. 26 Closing Interactions by Client Type

Client Type	Closing Interaction (Phone vs. Face-to-Face)	Priming Question or Statement for Closing Meeting	Areas to Reinforce (Spoken Words)	Areas to Avoid
Newly Married Professional Couple	Whichever is most convenient for them, but face-to-face is preferred, as they are busy people and many things are new again	• Statement • Their world is buzzing. Be a confident, calming factor.	• Where they feel less vulnerable • What they have accomplished thus far	• Additional personal finance/ relationship issues that may not be settled at this stage
Local Fortune 500 Employer	Face-to-face with your team, as they need to know you understand their employee base and have the resources to deliver	• Question • You want to reaffirm their vision providing employee benefits and to see if anything has changed.	• How they are leveraging benefits to support morale • Retention • Performance • Expectations of a provider	• Negotiating fees in the final meeting
Recently Displaced Executive	Face-to-face because this is a tough time for these folks, as they need to be kept busy working a plan	• Statement • Let them redirect if you are off base.	• Their input in the process • The uptick in the job market • The control they will have ongoing	• Questions about their job search process because they may not have made much progress
Retired, Looking for Income	Face-to-face because this is all about trust, facing the unknown, and committing to action	• Statement • This person needs focus and confidence.	• Their excitement around plans for retirement • Lifestyle ambitions and wealth transfer goals	• Health issues unless they offer insights
CEO of a Small Firm (Sitting in Cash)	Face-to-face or phone because they are busy so get them when you can. Know their business model inside and out, and sell the value of your recommendations.	• Question • CEOs know where they are and where they want to go.	• Future growth plans • Community activity • Recent wins	• Minor execution details • Problems in their business

Closing Lore

A lot has been written about closing, so much so that it stimulates a smirk just thinking about the topic. You've read all the books. And who can forget Alec Baldwin in *Glengarry Glen Ross*? I know I'll never think of "ABC" the same way again. But here we as salespeople find ourselves in what I call the "Fifth Decade of Selling" with an even greater need for prospect commitment.

In the seventies, product firms sold what they created, negotiated hard, and went out for a three-martini lunch. The eighties were all about the features and benefits sale that was too formulaic. The nineties were a breath of fresh air for clients in that advisors started asking questions. This led to a lot of Q & A burnout that some have described as death by questioning. We then arrived at our current state of selling (solution selling) with the arrival of the millennium, where product groups started creating solutions aligned with investor demand and an aging population. But the next decade of selling has to focus more on the client type and less on product. I call it the Decade of the Value Creator.

As for closing, the relationship and retention focus of wealth management firms over the last ten years has actually served to be the enemy of closing. With these firms feeling the need to protect valued clients and fend off competition, they focused on being consultative. But consultative morphed into being too nice and too careful not to sell.

At ProDirect, we feel relationship building and closing need to (and can) coexist. This next generation of selling has got to be about mutual value creation. It's not about your product or platform anymore. Anyone still standing after the recent recession has good product. High-performing advisors are winning by trading on their insights, provocative views of the prospect's landscape, and a passionate point of view on how clients should be viewing that reality. It's about wearing the client's world like a second skin, that is, to be intellectually curious about problems and opportunities for their client type. High-performing advisors are also masters at orchestrating the right resources at the right time to give everyone in the process comfort to move forward.

So how did we get here? An informal ProDirect survey of branch managers conducted recently revealed that, in over 75 percent of client and prospect interactions, advisors were not closing on an outcome. What's more important, the survey notes that nearly 90 percent of opportunities aren't closing as forecasted.

The reasons leaders in wealth management give for these low close rates are many, but a few themes ring out:

- "fear of damaging the relationship if my people push too hard"

- "lack of clarity around what the client really wants"

- "not enough engagement from the prospect in the process"

As a result, advisors have found themselves in a state of stagnation versus one of advancement with prospects and clients. Without high levels of engagement early in the sales process, more and more prospects are procrastinating and not returning phone calls. Plus, the latest recession made people fall in love with the status quo or made them too paralyzed with fear to decide or change. With a need for revenue, many advisors started falling back to their old ways of selling product, sensing it was more tangible to them and their clients. What that promoted were dialogues focused on pitches with clients saying "Nope, that's not it" over and over again.

Other factors are impacting close rates as well. Here's a list of common mistakes:

- e-mailing a proposal without a firm commitment to review it with a prospect

- incessant calls to the prospect to check in

- too much work on the part of the prospect to get started (for example, firm diagnostic tools)

- lack of a response to indifference, such as "I need to think about it"

- poor diagnosis of change and client types yielding the wrong conversations

At ProDirect, we've isolated six specific behaviors critical to improving closing effectiveness.

1. **Planning:** This is about setting a specific commitment objective that you'd like your prospect to agree to. It's built from your sleuthing and the impact of your last interaction.

2. **Client Type Openings:** In starting client type-specific conversations, your opening must link your objective to this type, such as a recently displaced executive, newly married professional couple, or small business owner looking to expand. This also anchors the purpose of your meeting, which feels more relevant to the prospect.

3. **Surfacing the Problem:** Teeing up a problem is about introducing an issue unique to a client type that the prospect identifies with. It could be dissatisfaction with the current state or some constructive discontent with his or her current portfolio. In the case of a recently displaced executive, you know that this person will be in a job search that will require him or her to use time productively and to keep a positive outlook.

4. **Solution "Options":** High-performing advisors offer several solution recommendations come closing time. This is where advisors provide several viable options tied to the problem surfaced earlier. Good closers offer these options directly matched to the prospect's input on the problems that were teed up.

5. **Solicit Opinions:** It's always tempting to move right to the close after offering up your solution. But the best FAs hold out a little longer. They know you'd rather have spoken concerns now than months full of unreturned phone calls. By asking for feedback from the prospect on your recommendations, you further validate the individual, and you know where you stand. Never ask "What do you think?" ever. The prospect's response will be too limiting. Ask for opinions and points of view instead.

6. **Close on a Commitment:** The close as a behavior ties back to the commitment objective you set out for the prospect and includes a recap of the specific client type/problem/solution that

you identified together. Closing is not something you do to a prospect. Rather, it's something you achieve together. If it feels like you're the one doing the closing, go back to earlier dialogues where you had high prospect buy-in and start over. And always review the progress you've made together and request a mutually beneficial action. Remember, you've earned this moment, and it's your time too.

The Heart of the Close: Bringing It All Together with CPS

CPS (client type/problem/solution) is the core of the conversation that gets the close done. It's a mapping of the problems that various client types encounter with several solutions. As you're presenting this to a prospect, noted author John Orvos tells salespeople to think of it as a hurt-and-rescue mission. Your research is telling you about the client type and the hurt he or she is experiencing. The rescue is the solution that matches up best to a corresponding client problem.

To be more effective at closing, it's all about the setup. Closing has to mimic prospects' thinking, so I advise clients to prepare for and execute dialogues that have a CPS structure at their core. But why is this always harder than we think? Because we want to appear knowledgeable to our prospects. We want to have the ready answer to a problem. We want to close the sale. But rushing too quickly to a solution has an opposite, negative effect. Prospects will actually see you as less credible than you actually are. High net worth prospects need to be validated. They're smart people. They've experienced success, and most likely, they'll want to think things through.

**Closing has to mimic prospects' thinking.
Conduct meetings that have a CPS structure at their core.**

Let's look at CPS in more detail.

- **C—Client Type:** The C is a targeted opening based on a specific client type your prospect falls into, a retired CFO, for example. This opening should also speak to what you discovered in your preparation or what your last interaction revealed about what's important to this person and those like him or her.

- **P—Problem:** The P is about the problems or uniqueness of a prospect situation. While every prospect's situation is unique, there are identifiable patterns of interest based on what folks do and how they interact with their wealth. By acknowledging the prospect's relevant issues and by getting him or her to open up about them, it serves to drive greater engagement and to minimize procrastination. Why? Your eventual recommendation will be couched in the prospect's spoken words about these problems. Not addressing the prospect's problem is the number-one factor in procrastination.

- **S—Solution Options:** The S is about offering up several options based on what you learned in your problem tee-up discussion. Note that it's not one solution, but a series of two to three intelligent recommendations based on how CPS is shaping up thus far in the dialogue. Why more than one? Our experience suggests that, if you present only one solution, prospects think, "That's it? That's my only choice?" In a way, one solution at this stage of the interaction is too limiting, and your opportunity can stall.

Here are a few common client types spread out according to the CPS framework:

Fig. 27 The ProDirect CPS Grid

Client Type	Problems Associated with That Type	Potential Solutions
Newly Married Professional Couple	Multiple 401(k)s Redundant investments Heavily invested in equities	Asset allocation funds
Local Fortune 500 Employer	Investment vehicles for retirees	Hybrid index annuities
Recently Displaced CFO	Emotional loss Unsure future	Cash value life insurance

Retired	Looking for income	Equity income (multicap value)
		Diversity bond
CEO of a Small Firm (Sitting in Cash)	Wait and see	Ginnie Mae fund
	Looking for opportunity	Short-term government
		Diversity bond

Note the client types above, the problems these client types typically encounter, and a solution or two that lines up with that situation. You could probably fill in your own client types. Just make sure the problems with those types are fully articulated and the solutions to those problems match up well. If you have trouble completing the grid for your prospects, don't go it alone. Grab a thinking partner in your firm or one of your best clients, and flush a few of these out. Just make sure this work links back to the ideal client types you identified back in chapter 5.

Putting It All Together: The Closing Conversation

So let's revisit the closing behaviors outlined earlier and the way they connect to the prospect interaction. I've talked about the what. Now let's look at the how.

Planning

Strategic planning is about identifying the client type of the prospect, pulling forward any spoken words and insights from your last interaction, and forming a hypothesis on how you can help. While there is plenty written about the perfect way to prep for a sales call, I recommend a tactic that John Miller at Velocity LLC recommends. John's an accomplished coach and a friend of the firm. He finds it helpful for his clients to answer four questions as part of the closing planning and prep process:

From your *last* interaction:

1. What did I achieve, and what is the current opportunity with this prospect?

2. What did I learn that needs to be considered for the next interaction?

For your *next* interaction:

3. What is my goal for this meeting? What do I want to gain commitment on?

4. How will I achieve my goal (a plan for each step of the meeting)?

As part of your meeting prep, forward your agenda in advance to the prospect, and get some feedback on it. Typically, four to five items are best. In your e-mail, simply ask the prospect to add or subtract from the agenda you've suggested and confirm the logistics of the meeting. I'm amazed at how often a prospect says, "Looks good. See you then." It sounds like a minor point but you're getting the engagement train rolling early.

Client Type Meeting Opening

To open the closing call effectively, exchange pleasantries in your own personality. But directly after that, anchor the meeting with a priming statement that speaks to the prospect's client type (for example, recently displaced executive) and the ideas you've come prepared to share. This is also a great time to briefly review the agenda. If this sounds like Sales 101, it is. But I am shocked at how many advisor meetings I shadow don't include this valuable step. Most often, the agenda you bring is what the prospect takes notes on!

Highly coveted prospects expect to receive immediate benefit from the effort of meeting with you. Your job is to connect them to your last interaction, express that you have been listening to them, and, as a result, have a few items to review. Here's another way to look at it.

The prospect's needs treadmill is already running. You need to match speed and get up there with him or her. Even if it's your first meeting, build upon the sleuthing you did with the person who referred you so you get a sense of the prospect's challenges.

The prospect's needs treadmill is already running. You need to match speed and get up there with him or her.

The goal of the client type opening is to engage the prospect in the first six seconds to make the rationale of meeting explicit and valuable. We call this opening a Client Type Opening (C) because it's just that. It addresses a client type that your prospect can immediately identify with. Here, we use the RVT format introduced earlier to level set the closing conversation.

SAMPLE Client Type Opening (Rationale, Value, Test):

R: *During our last meeting, we agreed that an important goal for retired clients like you needing income is an investment with moderate upside with no risk to principal.*

V: *Today, I thought we could discuss how Equity-Indexed Annuities can pay a base return that may be higher if the index increases. You won't fully participate in all of the gains when the market increases, but you also won't lose any principal in a falling market.*

T: *Does this sound like time well spent?*

In this example, you're making a connection to the last interaction, one that featured the discovery of a need for a retiree needing modest growth from a portion of his or her portfolio. The advisor in this case is anchoring the thrust of the meeting, focusing it on solutions to generate the needed income.

Here is another example of a client type meeting opening:

R: *Regarding our previous conversation on young professional couples with multiple 401(k)s/locations . . .*

V: *I have some ideas and data around the perception that multiple plans in multiple places doesn't mean asset allocation.*

T: *There are probably many other problems we can discuss related to 401(k) consolidation, but I thought this would be a good starting point for us based on our last few discussions.*

This example also connects a prospect to a prior interaction and a potential need for an asset allocation solution.

Problem Tee-Up

Coming out of the client type opening, you've piqued the client's interest and are prepared to discuss a particular problem. At this stage, problem tee-up is about expanding and clarifying the importance of an issue that you're uniquely prepared to address.

Prospects don't want to hear a pitch. In fact, they listen for your understanding of their issues and your capacity to do something about them. Hopefully, that something is different and better than what they're getting from their current advisor.

So the problem tee-up step helps you do that and more. What I've learned from our postmortem debriefs with advisors is that most opportunities have stalled due to client procrastination and a belief that that status quo is better than changing. The problem tee-up helps you qualify the nature and intensity of a prospect's problem so you can address it as well as determine if he or she is worth the effort. Prospects are more likely to move forward when they hear that you have experience with folks like them and are well versed in their problems with a track record in helping others. Proper execution of the problem tee-up allows you to acknowledge a problem from the client's point of view and should be something you know your product can closely service or solve.

Problem Tee-Up Examples

So, Mike, we've been talking about someone like you in retirement looking for income. People are living longer, right? Well, the problem I'm seeing is that investors aren't always sure how much income they actually need and over what time frame. Can you tell me more about what you see as your unique challenge around this?

- In this example, you're trying to establish the prospect's view of how much is enough for his vision of retirement. It can set you up for a recommendation to put a plan in place to reach a milestone or to explore more deeply the prospect's perception or frustration with a gap.

Here's what we're seeing with physicians coming together to form care group networks. In this situation, they need comp and benefits for their associates and another tier for themselves. The job is delegated to a committee that has to make the decision for everyone, which can be daunting. How is the process working for you and your team presently? What's been the hardest part?

- More and more physicians are operating in groups. Beyond obvious economies of scale, physicians are also joining these groups to support their financial goals now and when they retire. These professionals are not equipped to make these decisions, ones often hampered by internal consensus-driven decision processes. Without the problem tee-up step, your pitch will be perceived as too final too soon, which can lead to prospect procrastination.

Without the Problem Tee-up step, your pitch will be perceived as too final too soon. This leads to prospect procrastination.

Look at some of the client types and associated problems in figure 28. For any client type you encounter, you can gain valuable input to drive dialogues that put you in a position to recommend your solution.

Fig. 28 The Client Type/Problem/Solution Framework (CPS)

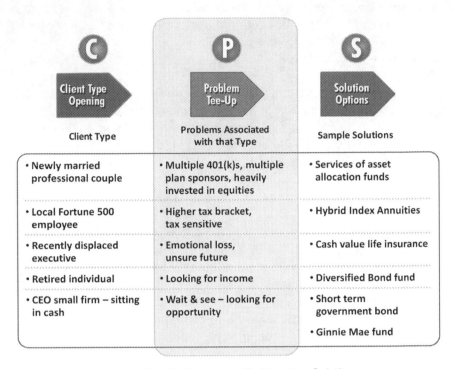

Client Type	Problems Associated with that Type	Sample Solutions
• Newly married professional couple	• Multiple 401(k)s, multiple plan sponsors, heavily invested in equities	• Services of asset allocation funds
• Local Fortune 500 employee	• Higher tax bracket, tax sensitive	• Hybrid Index Annuities
• Recently displaced executive	• Emotional loss, unsure future	• Cash value life insurance
• Retired individual	• Looking for income	• Diversified Bond fund
• CEO small firm – sitting in cash	• Wait & see – looking for opportunity	• Short term government bond
		• Ginnie Mae fund

Connecting the Prospect's Problem to a Solution

The other benefit of the problem tee-up is that it helps you capture the spoken words and opinions of your prospect. These words are what you'll include as you couch your final, intelligent recommendation. Remember, clients love to hear their name in lights.

Solution Options

This step is about delivering your solution in the context of the credibility you've engendered in your meeting thus far. If you've followed the CPS process, you've primed a conversation specific to a client type, surfaced corresponding problems (problem tee-up) for that client type, and validated the prospect by capturing his or her point of view of the problem. Now you are ready to talk solution.

In my closing process, I recommend two to three solutions that are appropriate for the client type problem scenario you identify. The goal of presenting multiple solutions goes a little beyond the obvious. You want the prospect to take an active role in the process of creating the solution that's best for him or her, one that aligns with what he or she said about the problem. High-performing advisors are successful in closing because they strive for engagement early and often with their prospects.

There are two aspects to the solution options step:

1. **Solution:** Offer your solution recommendation based on your problem tee-up.

2. **Check:** Check agreement and stimulate dialogue on the options you presented.

Here's an example of how it might sound:

Solution and Check Example

Solution: *So, Mike, based on the world of the retired CFO and the issues you are facing, I would recommend the Equity Income Fund in order to give you a conservative equity fund with quarterly income plus a way to diversify your growth investments.*

Check: *How close does this match up to some of the issues you've been pondering as a potential path forward?*

In this example, the advisor validated the retired CFO prospect by demonstrating knowledge in the issues he is facing as well as paying deference to the research the prospect may be already doing on his own. It's likely that the change type of this prospect is a Tiger.

Best practice also shows that checking for agreement on each option before going to the next solution recommendation helps to further stave off prospect procrastination. Presenting all solutions in batch mode makes it hard for the prospect to process all the details and form specific questions. By securing incremental commitment versus one big sale at the end, you create interest about the value in the next step in the sales process.

Soliciting Opinions

In chapter 1, we talked about closing as an engagement game. It's important to get a prospect's feedback on your recommendation as often as possible in the sales discussion. These spoken words are gold. Most advisors blow right by this step. Right after you present your solutions to the problem tee-up you surfaced, you have to get some feedback. Believe me when I say that a wealthy investor *will* have a point of view. The Soliciting Opinions step is a more professional way of doing a trial close. It's about eliciting an opinion on your solution options for the specific client type based on points of agreement thus far in your meeting. It also provides you an opportunity to manage any resistance now and determine if the prospect has any unspoken objections. Most of the time, this feedback is very valuable and useful in shaping your ultimate recommendation.

Soliciting Opinions: Seeking Clarity

Here are some questions to use when soliciting opinions from customers and prospects. From my research, I've found that resistance typically comes from four areas:

1. A gap between the need and the solution

2. Confidence in the advisor

3. Comfort in the process and approach

4. Decision support from peers or family

So no matter what the nature of the resistance, you can find your way through it. Based on the nature of the resistance, you always have a specific next step.

Let Me Think about It

Before we move on, let me address a common objection at this stage of the sales process, "Let me think about it." If you've been tracking with the Designing Conversations process, I suggest that you check in with your prospect at each step. This keeps concerns or reservations from building up and makes the closing process a lot easier for both of you at the end.

I have several advisor clients that tell prospects up front that this is a mutual discovery process and you are both investing time in seeking a fit. These advisors tell prospects to be honest and open with how they are feeling or if they would articulate any concerns as you both move through the process. You may still have prospects that will remain tight-lipped, but it can be helpful to put the notion out there. Be genuinely respectful, concerned, and open. Prospects rarely have a problem with that.

Here are some proven responses to the request for time to think about it:

1. "This is your financial future. You should make a good decision. How would you like me to support you in the process?" Ask the prospect if he or she would share his or her decision process with you.

2. "I understand how you are feeling about the recommendations we came to at present. Is there anything missing that you were looking for?" If a gap exists, identify it, and ask what it would take to close it.

3. "Based on what you shared with me and what we uncovered together, what would give you an even higher level of comfort in my recommendations at this time?" Ask for perceived pros and cons from the prospect.

4. "How would you gauge the comfort level of all decision-makers involved in the solutions that were recommended?" Invite all members of a decision-making body to speak to your reference clients or review current trends in the area of your recommendations.

Let's look at these types of resistance and some of the actions you can take to advance the sale:

-   **Solution Gap:** The prospect perceives something as missing in your offering. Or your competition is offering an actual factor that you aren't.

- **Confidence:** Here you want to ensure that the prospect feels that your approach is sound and you can deliver.

- **Comfort:** The prospect needs to feel comfortable with your process and his or her own decision making. One of the biggest fears investors have is the fear of making the wrong decision. Make them feel that they've left no stone unturned and you are the right choice. Most people have a confidant or trusted advisor they turn to for big decisions. Encourage that for your prospect.

- **Support:** In some cases, it's helpful to ask what additional support you can provide to help the prospect make his or her best decision. If you're selling to a committee where more than one person is involved, it may help to provide the prospect with tools or job aids to help him or her inform his or her peers. One of our advisor clients was asked to be on speakerphone during a board meeting in case any questions came up.

Another thing that can happen is that other agendas emerge. This could happen in a family scenario or when selling to a committee when someone is not aligned. Or worse yet, there can be instances when someone will actually attempt to derail your recommendations. In this case, you should offer to meet with this person. If you do not do this step well, it becomes another product pitch, and the prospect will tune out and likely ask for *more* time to think about it.

So at this point, I've been writing a lot about the valuable parts of a closing conversation. Here's how a closing conversation might actually sound. Note the CPS triggers in each of the steps.

During our last meeting, we agreed that an important goal for CFOs in transition is a good allocation plan for their severance package with enough liquidity for a prolonged job search. Today, I thought we could discuss how when designed properly, a cash value life insurance policy can provide income in a tax-efficient manner, while also providing growth, asset protection, and a death benefit. Does this sound like time well spent?

We also talked about your current employment situation. CFO job turnover is really slow, right? Well, the problem I'm seeing is that investors in your shoes aren't always sure how much liquidity they actually need over the span of a job search. Can you tell me more about what you see as your personal challenge around this?

Well, Mike, based on your situation and others in the same boat, I would recommend the Compass Fund or Tremont Equity Income in order to give you a conservative equity fund with quarterly income and a way to diversify your growth investments. Can you see the connection to what you were looking for?

Based on what I've shared with you thus far, how on track am I with my recommendation? How would you rate your level of confidence in the approach at this point? What can I provide to help you make a decision you're really comfortable with?

So to sum it up, we've been talking about prudent investment options for recently displaced executives like yourself. Our focus has been on the importance of providing income during a job search while providing for sound asset allocation. You felt that it was a good idea to look to bonds for a solution, and our Equity Income Fund seems to fit the bill. At this point, I feel you've shared so much with me, and together, we've left no stone unturned. Can I ask for your authorization to purchase XX shares of the Equity Income Fund today so we can get started?

By following this process, you increase your chances of achieving your commitment objective for the call because you've driven a high level of prospect engagement. Getting prospects to talk about their situation or problem gives you fodder to calibrate your recommendation using their spoken words. When you offer your solution, I love to hear advisors say, "Based on what you shared with me about you and your situation, I believe I can help."

Other Support for Your Closing: Procrastination

One of the things we all know as salespeople is that procrastination is the prospect's wonderful prerogative. Sometimes what we compete with is not just another advisor or another firm, but the prospect's choice of doing nothing. In some cases, making a decision can actually represent loss to the prospect: loss of control, loss of what is known, or loss of the choice to make a future decision (once they've made it).

As Tony Robbins, the celebrated motivational speaker, puts it, "We have two intrinsic human motivations: one is to avoid pain and the other is to seek pleasure." In that light, it's helpful to understand how your prospect perceives moving to another advisor and another firm. In chapter 5, we talked a lot about change types and how certain prospects view change.

On the Tony Robbins "avoid pain" side, many prospects feel that making a change will be a total time drain because of the need to assemble documents, track down account numbers, and so forth. For others, it's coming off autopilot from their current advisor to get a new one up to speed. It's very reasonable for the prospect to feel he or she won't be cared for in the same way in the new firm because he or she is new. These factors can all lead to delayed decisions or stalled opportunities.

What's important in your early dialogues with prospects is to get a sense of the big decisions they've made lately. Here are a few sample questions to use:

- Can you tell me about your decision to sell your company? What was your process? What did you wrestle with the most?

- What's the biggest nonfinancial decision that you've made for your family in the last year? How did you get to the end result?

- Where do you get your best counsel around the decisions that need to be made in your business?

- If we had the chance to work together, how might you want me to support you in your decision-making process?

While advisors know how many meetings have been held, what was said, and what the logical next step is, prospects really aren't sure. They're busy managing their business, their life, and their family. In the case of more complex sales such as retirement planning for employers, often the best value an advisor can provide is letting the prospect know where he or she is and the tangible value of taking the next step.

Closing on a Commitment

I was having lunch with a managed accounts consultant one day. I was running a training class for his group, and he was so excited to get back to his office for a meeting he had scheduled for Monday. He said to me, "Man, I can't wait to get back home. I have a meeting with a prospect, and he's got forty million to convert to our platform. He really likes what he's seeing." Naturally I got excited too and started to ask a few questions, one of which was how many meetings he'd had with that prospect and what his progress looked like.

He took a bite of his sandwich, and I did the same. And then he said it. He started to put his tongue to the top of his teeth, like we all do when we're about to say a word that starts with "th." I thought for sure he was going to say "three." What do you think he said?

He said, "Thirteen."

That night, the Relationship Review tool was born.

To support advisors in their closing effort, I've created the Relationship Review tool, a guided process that conveys to your prospect the value you've both created over time, key milestones achieved, and any concerns that were addressed to the prospect's satisfaction. The tool is as much a progress tracker as it is a conversation to reaffirm with your prospect that you've left no stone unturned and you both possess the information and insight to proceed at this time.

Why is that important? As salespeople, we are constantly looking at the pipeline and the notes in our CRM system. Our prospects aren't. We know what happened on the last call, where we'd like to go on the next, and how many meetings we've had in between. The prospect isn't tracking this. To keep procrastination at bay, you must keep the path you've taken and the cumulative agreements achieved front and center constantly. Prospects might remember the last few meetings, but most aren't keeping a running tally of the value you're establishing on their behalf. If you add any additional anxiety around change to that, the memory can cloud further.

To keep procrastination at bay, keep the path you've taken and the cumulative agreements achieved front and center constantly.

Alternative investments, separately managed accounts, and deferred compensation plans all carry their own degree of complexity with them. As a result, I see the sales process for many advisors becoming lengthy and disjointed.

With more moving parts and the need for deeper levels of prospect understanding, many sales opportunities are stalling as a result. In the case of these more complex sales, often the best value an advisor can provide is letting the prospect know where he or she is and the tangible value of taking the next step. The Relationship Review tool does just that.

Fig. 29 The Relationship Review Tool

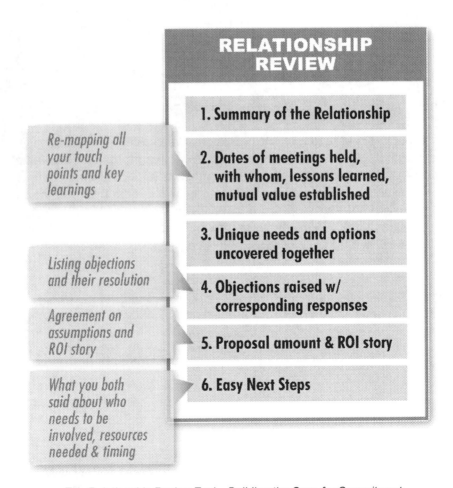

The Relationship Review Tool—Building the Case for Commitment

This tool is not meant to be filled out and sent or shown to your prospect to show him or her up. Rather, it's a conversation guide and support visual that speaks to what you and the prospect have accomplished together. Let's drill down on each part of the tool:

1. **Summary of the Relationship:** This is two to three sentences that speak to how you met, the purpose of the dialogue, and a nod to the client type/problem/solution framework.

2. **Contact Management:** This is a credibility and momentum builder that shows how much work you've both put in. Capture the dates of meetings held and with whom, discussion topics, lessons learned, and any mutual value established.

3. **Unique Needs Uncovered:** This is what settled out of your meetings for both you and the prospect that supports the foundation of your eventual recommendation. It's the combination of full client type identification and associated problem exploration. You will use this insight as you make your final recommendations for the prospect.

4. **Objections and Your Responses:** Similar to step two, this is a credibility builder for you in that you're listing all the objections that were raised and their corresponding responses. This reinforces once more that you've left no stone unturned. You also want to validate the prospect by letting her know you heard her and empathize with her concerns. Whether you received an innocent misperception or more forceful skepticism, you don't want to open the door to any more resistance than you have to.

5. **Investment Recommendations:** This is the dollar figure and deliverables you've recommended to your prospect. Take the opportunity to spell out any unique requirements or differentiated value-adds.

6. **Easy Next Steps:** By going through this process, you've earned the right to suggest an easy next step. State simply what needs to be done next, and reaffirm the value of doing so. Reflect that both of you have come a long way together and, in your experience, you have enough to move forward.

Steps two and four are the most critical in the Relationship Review process. It shows that you've listened to the prospect and your level of detail makes it hard for a prospect to argue with the recommendations you've arrived at together.

Review and Request

So now you have to be asking, "What are the magic words I should say to close the deal?" While the words are important, it's the way in which you ask for commitment to your final recommendation that will make the difference. I recommend an approach I call Review and Request. Similar to what you captured in your Relationship Review tool, you're summarizing your process thus far and asking for the next best action that gains the prospect's commitment.

Review

John, during our discussions about prudent investment options for consideration by the American Cancer Society board, we focused on the importance of avoiding investments in companies deemed harmful by the organization. Based on their performance and avoidance of tobacco companies, you felt that our Socially Responsible Funds might be an ideal fit.

Request

I'd love to work with you in satisfying the board's goal of working these funds into their portfolio. Can I get your commitment to review the prospectus with the board at their next monthly meeting?

Review

Sandra, one of the dominant themes from our discussions has been your need for an exit strategy from your business. You want to make sure you have enough put away for retirement but retain a portion of the proceeds to invest in another business. We thought that putting a portion of your investible capital in iShares provides a targeted sector investment at a high level of liquidity. As you know, iShares can be bought and sold throughout the trading day.

Request

To build a diversified portfolio right now, I recommend we buy the S&P 500 Index Fund (symbol: IVV). It's a single commission transaction that gives us the flexibility we're looking for. I have your fax number. Let me send over the account opening form for your signature, and we can get this taken care of in the next twenty-four hours.

If these examples seem a little assertive or salesy, remember that, at this stage, you've done so much work on behalf of the prospect that you've earned the right to be direct.

Please keep in mind that the request at this point is not an assumptive close. All that you're doing is being in service to your prospect and taking accountability for the next best action. Be firm and direct in asking for what you want. At this stage of the process, it's likely the right thing to do.

CHAPTER 10

PUTTING THE FOUR-HEADED DRAGON
PROCESS INTO PRACTICE

My goal for this chapter is to help you anchor the key points in the Taming model and chart valuable tactics to help you get closer to your goals. Hopefully you've got a list of good takeaways to support your journey of meaning more to clients and prospects. It's not an easy task to manage existing clients, attract more prospects, maintain a reputation, and handle all the admin that goes with it. But the best get it done. High-performing advisors know they have limited time to focus on growth, and they can't afford to be bad at it. And that's why I wrote this book.

By now, you've learned at least four things: the right goal is liberating, a clear picture of your ideal prospect is ideal, a good value prop fuels prospecting, and making contact is an art and a science. In reading this book, I hope you've found useful tools and feel I spoke to your unique situation.

Fig. 30 Taming the Four-Headed Dragon (The Model)

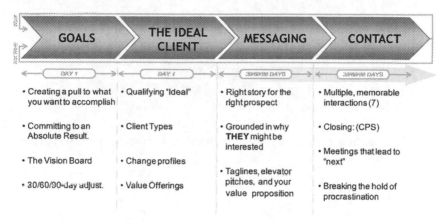

Taming the Four-Headed Dragon Model

The following is a list of best practices from each step of the Taming the Four-Headed Dragon system we've covered together.

Goals

- **Practice 1:** Set them. Craft one absolute result for the year that you can commit to, one that will create maximum leverage for the growth of your practice.

- **Practice 2:** Choose visuals that represent what you want to accomplish and why. Create a vision board and keep it in eyeshot where you do your best work.

- **Practice 3:** Rely less on administrative systems, spreadsheets, and planners.

- **Practice 4:** Be good to yourself if you fall off track with your progress. Self-criticism will dilute your efforts.

- **Practice 5:** Adjust your plan every ninety days.

- **Practice 6:** Test your goals with people who know you.

- **Practice 7:** Help others set good goals. The best advisors are coaches.

- **Practice 8:** We speak at 125 words per minute, but we think at 450. Think your goals. What you focus on grows.

- **Practice 9:** Forget lengthy to-do lists. Create a Big Six list each day. You'll have less carryover.

- **Practice 10:** For anything you want to accomplish, make sure you can articulate why.

The Ideal Client

- **Practice 1:** Sketch a picture of your ideal client. Include as much detail as possible.

- **Practice 2:** Consider criteria other than AUM, such as respect for your time, courtesy, and openness to new ideas.

- **Practice 3:** Use the ideal client profile tool to assess your best fit. Total scores of forty-five to fifty are near perfect.

- **Practice 4:** Make sure prospects understand and appreciate your process.

- **Practice 5:** Understand a client's orientation toward change. The best prospects are with someone else. Tigers and Eager Beavers are ideal.

- **Practice 6:** Work your ideal client profile into referral requests, and educate your network.

- **Practice 7:** Assess prospects' appetites for detail, especially if that's your forte.

- **Practice 8:** Contrast your ideal client with the bottom 10 percent of your book. Weed out those clients you're tolerating (high maintenance and low respect).

- **Practice 9:** Write out an ideal client declaration, and send it to all your contacts. Put the vibration out there.

- **Practice 10:** Recognize that you are a dynamic being. Over time, your view of who is ideal may and will change. You will change.

Messaging

- **Practice 1:** Recognize that effective messaging will come from your best clients. Ask them what they value in the relationship, and fashion that into your value proposition.

- **Practice 2:** Avoid jargon. The most successful clients have heard it all before, and if they don't get it, they won't tell you.

- **Practice 3:** Test your messaging at conferences, networking events, and social outings. Note what people connect with. This is especially true for your tagline.

- **Practice 4:** Your I/Why/You pitch should include why others specifically choose you as their advisor.

- **Practice 5:** Align your messaging with a client type and a corresponding problem. Your messaging should speak to who you help, what problems you solve, and which visions you enable for clients.

- **Practice 6:** Based on the client type, the YOU portion of your elevator pitch needs to speak to why you think the prospect would be interested in meeting with you.

- **Practice 7:** Visit the website of other advisor firms and see how they talk about themselves. Most all sound the same. Would you be interested if you were a prospect? Take the best of all of them and forge your own web presence.

- **Practice 8:** Without making specific claims, describe the impact of your involvement on clients' personal and business objectives.

- **Practice 9:** Stay current in your reading. Your messaging must be at or slightly ahead of current events and trends in the market.

- **Practice 10:** Use your messaging everywhere—websites, letterhead, e-mail signatures, business cards, and meeting agendas (within compliance regulations, of course).

Contact and Closing

- **Practice 1:** You must earn the right for referrals. If someone is not familiar with your work, ask for an introduction instead.

- **Practice 2:** Anyone who is worth contacting will not be easy to reach. Make your seven touches varied and valuable.

- **Practice 3:** There is no one best way to reach a prospect. E-mail, fax, blog, FedEx, LinkedIn, and snail mail are all viable options when orchestrated well and with purpose.

- **Practice 4:** In all cases, suggest an agenda, and get early feedback on it. This starts the engagement pathway with your prospect.

- **Practice 5:** Trade on the special needs, knowledge, and insights you bring to prospects. Everyone, including your competition, has product.

- **Practice 6:** The CPS framework (client type, problem, solution framework) is your guide for messaging and recommending solutions. Follow the CPS framework for all meetings, contact, and closing.

- **Practice 7:** For any meeting, anchor it with a priming statement, and use pebble and payoff questions to clarify what's important for your prospect.

- **Practice 8:** Solicit the prospect's spoken words about his or her view of perfection and what he or she stands to gain by achieving it. Get your prospect to tell you the value of doing something about it.

- **Practice 9:** Closing is never a clever quip or catchphrase, and there is no silver bullet. It's a process driven by a client type problem conversation process that puts you in position to make an intelligent recommendation.

- **Practice 10:** Use your Relationship Review tool to inform prospects of the value you've created together, and let them know that you're both ready to decide after thorough analysis. Review all that you've accomplished, and request a mutually beneficial next action.

We've covered a lot of ground together in this book. The intent of sharing the content and the Taming the Four-Headed Dragon system with you was to help you grow your practice for all the right reasons. We all have limited time for prospecting, and managing the four-headed dragon is an everyday reality. Advisors will always be faced with balancing their efforts with existing clients, prospects, their thought leadership, and the administration necessary to keep track of it all. The best know where their leverage lies, and hopefully you've found some for yourself over the last several chapters. You can make these dragons work together to maximize the impact you have on your clients and prospects. That's my aspiration for you.

Our experience working with advisors tells us that your prospects and clients will appreciate your disciplined and creative approach. Your reference base is eager to help you and will value having a great story to tell. This process should also validate all over again why you got into this business and the joy you have in helping people. Thank you for your interest and trust going forward.

Let me leave you with a quote from the late Steve Jobs, someone who never let his dragons stand in the way of his creativity and vision. "You have to trust in something—your gut, destiny, life, karma, whatever. This approach has never let me down, and it has made all the difference in my life."

Good luck, and good selling!

BIBLIOGRAPHY

- Dagher, Veronica. June 9, 2013. "Tweeting 101 for Financial Advisers." WSJ.com. http://online.wsj.com/news/articles/SB10001424 12788732480980457851124078638744.

- Davis, Clarky. February 15, 2011. "Commingling Your Finances: When Love and Money Come Together." CareOne Debt Relief Services web blog. http://community.careonecredit.com/b/careone_debt_discussions/archive/2011/02/15/commingling-your-finances-when-love-and-money-come-together.aspx.

- Haefele, Stacey. September 16, 2013. "Targeting Wealthy Clients: Understand Their Source of Wealth." Financial-Planning.com web blog. http://www.financial-planning.com/blogs/targeting-wealthy-clients-understand-their-source-of-wealth-26866181.html?ET=finan cialplanning:e15150:47760a:&st=email&utm_source=editorial&utm_medium=email&utm_campaign=FP_Wealth__100913.

- O'Connell, Brian. June 10, 2013. "How Financial Advisors are Using Social Media." Investopedia web article. http://www.investopedia.com/articles/professionals/061013/how-financial-advisors-are-leveraging-social-media.asp.

- Orvos, John. *The Four Faces of Sales*. Indianapolis, IN: iUniverse, 2013.

- Palomino, Jose. *Value Prop*. Philadelphia, PA: Cody Rock Press, 2008.

- Sitnick, Amy. July 16, 2013. "Why Facebook Rocks for Financial Advisors." Financial Social Media web article. http://financialsocialmedia.com/why-facebook-rocks-for-financial-advisors/.

- Sofia, Robert. April 3, 2013. "8 Things Financial Advisors Should Know About Social Media Compliance." Platinum Advisor Strategies web article. http://platinumstrategies.com/2013/04/03/8-things-financial-advisors-should-know-about-social-media-compliance/.

- Stanley, Thomas J. *Selling to the Affluent*. New York, NY: McGraw Hill, 1991.

- Thull, Jeff. *The Prime Solution*. Chicago, IL: Dearborn Trade Publishing, 2005.

AUTHOR'S NOTE

One of the goals I had in writing this book was to make it a continuous go-to resource for your work with prospects and clients. I provided a number of tools and worksheets to help you in your planning and framing the right conversations at the right time.

I invite you to go to www.4headeddragon.com for electronic copies of our tools as well as to participate in a running dialogue around the four dragons and prospect conversion. Check our calendar of events for a list of events, coaching calls, and special interest webinars as we look to support you beyond this book.

I value your feedback and interest in your professional growth and development.

ABOUT THE AUTHOR

Bill Walton is a nationally recognized sales trainer and coach with more than twenty-four years of experience helping individuals and teams mean more to clients. He is known for his cutting edge sales training and value proposition work with prominent Fortune 500 companies such as Prudential, American Express, and Merrill Lynch. Walton found particular success taking these same sophisticated selling techniques to the advisor-investor interaction. His own client work selling professional services spawned a consultative approach that has helped advisors drive greater conversion rates from their prospecting for more than thirteen years.

Walton takes a highly collaborative approach with his clients. The asset management and brokerage firms he's worked with have felt comfortable suggesting program ideas. In fact, his clients helped shape two of his turnkey programs for financial professionals—the 90-Day Dash and the Art of the Close.

The 90-Day Dash title was born from the work Walton was doing with early-stage companies. With limited resources—namely people and cash—these start-ups needed to have everyone on the team working together in one concentrated effort to drive revenue, "all hands on deck" if you will. Walton helped them harness all of their opportunity with a focused prospecting effort driven by the right goals, supported with crisp messaging, and guided by varied and valuable touches over ninety days.

The Art of the Close program was actually an outcropping of work he was doing with pharmaceutical reps to drive greater engagement with physicians. Walton rode with reps, sat in on opinion leader presentations, and listened to medical affairs executives tell him what they wanted from reps. This experience helped him create the CPS framework for deeper dialogues with really smart people that ends in a mutually beneficial next step.

Prior to founding ProDirect, Walton worked with Intro Inc. to incubate early-stage companies primed for unique market positions. While there, he built client value propositions, investor decks, and sales operations engines. Before Intro Inc., he worked for two prominent professional services firms selling large-scale sales training and consulting projects. His clients included CIGNA, Stanley Tools, and Unilever. During this time, he formulated his "meaning more to clients" philosophy of relationship management and learned what it took to add value to clients with extremely high expectations. Walton also spent ten years in sales and marketing within the consumer products industry, learning the value of delivering on a brand promise. These experiences have all served to provide the inspiration for his work with advisors today.

Walton publishes the Meaning More to Clients sales blog and has been a featured guest on CNN. He's worked as an adjunct professor at New York University and has been a featured contributor to *Human Resource Executive* magazine. Walton is an active member in the Professional Society of Sales and Marketing Trainers and the Greater Philadelphia Senior Executive Group (GPSEG) and currently sits on the board of the Juvenile Diabetes Research Foundation.

Walton graduated magna cum laude from Connecticut State University with a degree in business administration and received a master's degree in human resource education from Fordham University.